Praise
for
About The Voice of God

Chris Westhoff invites us into the sacred art of listening—not as a technique, but as a posture of surrendered attentiveness. In a noisy world obsessed with speaking, this book is a timely and profound reminder that transformation begins not with what we say, but with how we hear. Wise, grounded, and spiritually resonant—this is a must-read for anyone hungry to discern God's voice amid the clamor.

Danielle Strickland

Author, advocate, communicator

Chris Westhoff is a gift to the church. Her years of service and ministry have seasoned her voice; her book offers a valuable, authentic, and honest contribution to anyone seeking to understand the role and practice of the prophetic gift within the body of Christ today. Chris communicates with clarity, grace and wisdom to illuminate a complex and at times puzzling gift, and in doing so, inspires a hope filled desire to apply the teachings of this book in your own life.

Brian Heasley

International Prayer Director

24-7 Prayer

About the Voice of God is honest, insightful, substantial, and passionate. It is borne out of many years of experience and practice and comes from a person whose family, and friendships, bear the fruit of lives being well lived in the light of the voice of God. Christine and her husband Craig have been servants of God's church for many decades, blessing many thousands of people. This book continues in that vein and is worthy of being widely read.

Roger Ellis
Director
24-7 Communities Network

Christine writes with penetrating insight, wisdom and compassion born of her own courageous journey into the depths of God, the depths of her own soul, and her faithful accompaniment of others over decades. This book is a feast. Taste. Savour. It will both satisfy you and ignite deeper hunger.

Jill Weber
Director of Houses of Prayer
24/7 Prayer
Global Convenor, Order of the Mustard Seed

About *the* Voice *of* God

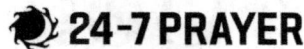
24-7 PRAYER

About The Voice of God
A Guide for the Journey

Copyright © 2025 Christine Westhoff

Published by

hawkeye.pro

Hawkeye.Pro
Nashville Tennessee

ISBN -13: 979-8-9913718-8-9 (Paperback)
ISBN -13 : 979-8-9913718-9-6 (Hardback)

Printed in the United States of America

Emphases in Scripture quotations added by the author.

About *the* Voice *of* God

A Guide for the Journey

Christine Westhoff

To Suzy Sammons (publisher and manager), my sister, dearest friend, and champion—thank you for believing in me, coaching me, and encouraging me every step of the way. Without your support, this book would not exist. I am deeply grateful.

My heartfelt gratitude also goes to Lori Janke, my editor, who believed in my voice from the outset and provided the strength to urge me onward.

And to 24-7 Prayer: You have been my global community for most of my adult life. Your friendship, leadership, and culture have shaped me in beautiful ways.

Thank you for receiving me.

Contents

Foreword

I remember, with some sympathy, my early days of trying to hear God's voice. Those days were filled with everything from awe and gratitude to frustration and bewilderment. I spent countless hours seeking to unearth the formulas, practices, and levers at my disposal to get responses when and how I wanted them. I hadn't yet learned His penchant for responding to my questions with His own questions or His appreciation for affectionate, provocative silence.

Without knowing it, I treated God far more like ChatGPT than a Father, seeking answers and information rather than self-disclosure and togetherness. It would become my most transformative journey.

When Christine and I connected for the first time, I quickly knew I'd discovered a friend on a kindred path. She was someone who had experienced the wonders of the things that prophetic people do and yet who had been softened and affectionately shaped by the longer road of allowing God into the deeper places. Those vulnerable places in which He is inclined to do His work if we'll give Him our "yes."

This ability to both experience and be experienced by God shouldn't be so rare, but it is. And this fact only makes friends like Christine all the more special to have. It also makes her a worthy companion to boldly and caringly lead us to discover God's voice.

Hearing God isn't as simple as it often sounds. Yes, we have Scripture, each other, and the witness of millenia of Christians before us, but to hear God personally and meaningfully involves no small amount of trust, persistence, and waiting. Of course, there are helpful practices that can foster these, but there are no risk-free formulas. Knowing and hearing God demands vulnerability precisely because communion isn't primarily functional, but personal.

I believe Christine will become as much of an encouragement to you as she has been to me as she beautifully articulates what it means for us to live that personal life with God.

About the Voice of God is not so much about the *science* of hearing God, but the *relationship*. Christine appeals to our humanity and the humanity of Christ, showing us how rich a relationship with the unseen One can truly be. As a well journeyed pilgrim herself, she offers practical tips, meditations, and reflections to help land the aetherial in the practical for the reader. But she also tells us what we often don't like to hear—that God's voice is mysterious, personal, confronting, and unfamiliar. She pushes against our need for quick fixes and easy answers and invites us to know the Person more than the proposition.

Christine hasn't only heard God's voice, she's *not* heard it, too, and that matters. Because as wonderful as the revelation and deep sense of God's *withness* we can experience is (and we're caringly led there in this book), we will all face our seasons of prolonged silence, confusion, and heartbreak. Christine's honesty and her time spent in the waiting place may just be her greatest qualifier to help us travel the deeper road of such a God-listening life.

What ultimately makes this such a special read is the wisdom held in these pages. Wisdom that comes from experience, from staying with it, from faithfulness, from years of reflection, and from helping us return to the One who loves us in every season. In Christine, we find a true guide, someone who knows what it means to scale the mountain *and* to be watered by the shadowed paths of the valley.

Reading this book felt like conversing with a friend who knows the same Spirit I do, the One who is deeply knowable and who is simultaneously whimsical and untamable. I was comforted to discover I'm not the only one who finds hearing God's voice more, not less, mysterious over time and yet is all the more enthralled because of it.

I pray that in the following pages you, too, will grow in sensitivity, affection, and adoring trust as you travel the road of learning about the voice of God.

Much love,
Strahan Coleman

Introduction
God Speaks

In the beginning, there was chaos. This is a tremendously encouraging thought. What if chaos often marks beginnings? We read in Genesis 1:2 that the earth was formless and void, there was darkness over the surface of the deep, and the Spirit of the Lord was hovering over it all. God saw the raw materials of darkness and deep formlessness and was inspired to paint, mold, craft, and create. Was it stormy? Were those waters stirred and raging, or were they dancing in anticipation? What *is* the darkness over the deep, and for that matter, what is the deep to which these words refer? This stunning poetic language leaves much to our imagination, which is really the point of poetry. Something existed before God brought order, and it was rather chaotic—much like my interior and exterior landscape feels some days. If you can relate, we can both breathe a sigh of relief knowing that the Holy Spirit is hovering. He seems to be attracted to chaos, which makes me think He's seeing something worthy, and even beautiful, woven through it all. As the storm raged and the darkness dominated, "God exhales, inspiring the void first with wind and then with the Word, which is both utterance and act, which makes something out of nothing by saying that it is so."[1]

In the beginning, God speaks. He also casually walks with His created ones through a garden made just for them. The hunger to hear His voice is intrinsic within every human being. It's woven through the DNA of the whole world, as if we can still sense the echo from His voice calling the dust into being. As He crafted the first human out of the dust of the earth, our every cell responded to the sound of His voice, the movement of His hands, and the breath of His lungs. I think our whole being still stands at attention waiting for His words. This life we live feels as if we are still walking in His garden, searching and longing for His company.

Learning to hear God's voice is an intensely nuanced conversation. We can too easily talk about it as if we can teach people a simple list of spiritual gymnastics to put into practice in order to learn a skill of some kind. When instead, it's an all-consuming, never-ending journey of opening our hearts to love and be loved, to see and be seen, to hold and be held.

The truth is that I'm less sure about His voice every year I walk this earth, and I think that's a good thing. I have been humbled, and my trusted tricks of the trade have all shattered around me. For this, I'm eternally grateful. Today, I would instinctively rebel against any quick formula for hearing Him or any attempt to package His voice in a prophetic-only box. I've been catapulted out of my overconfident spiritual techniques and thrown into a place where His mysterious nature has captured the core of my being.

---

1   Barbara Brown Taylor, *When God is Silent: Divine Language Beyond Words* (Canterbury Press, 2013), 12.

My presumption has been needfully confronted, but my awareness in His intimate involvement in our lives and our world is more secure and assured than ever. The landscape of mystery feels exciting and invitational, and the conversation about His voice is much more intimate and embodied. Today, I would describe any sense of perceiving God as being the opposite of concrete and closer akin to a wisp of wind or an illusive scent. There was a day that this concept would have caused me frustration because I was overly attached to utilitarian ways. Now, though, I relish the joy of the ineffable mystery of God's communication with humanity.

Hearing God's voice is not *really* hearing a voice, at least on most days. I understand there are stories in Scripture where we witness God speaking, so we can't ignore the possibility of His voice booming from the heavens. We read about Jesus praying, "'Father, glorify your name!' Then a voice came from heaven, 'I have glorified it, and will glorify it again'" (John 12:28 NIV). Many in the gathered crowd thought it had thundered, while others said an angel had spoken to Jesus. For those present, the experience of hearing seemed to be multifarious. The variety of ways God communicates with humans is more than the stars, and this puts an excited butterfly in my stomach, much like Christmas morning.

The voice of God is not synonymous with the prophetic. Within the prophetic gift and function is included (but not limited to) hearing God's voice. But in the same token, every time we hear God's voice doesn't mean that His words are prophetic. It's crucial that we distinguish between these two conversations for a wide variety of reasons.

One of the main reasons we exist is communion with God. The invitation offered to every human is intimate oneness with our Creator. We are hard-wired to hear, see, perceive, and commune with

Him. To confine God's communication within prophetic language feels constrictive, both to our intimate experience of communion with God and to the true purpose of the prophetic. They are two different conversations, and they both deserve their own day in the spotlight. The gift of prophecy has its own unique purpose and function in the world. This gift and grace of the Holy Spirit has a very specific mission regarding the fulfillment of the eternal purposes of Christ, which is no small matter. I have written in-depth on this topic in my other book entitled *Reframing the Prophetic*. We also have an immersive online course available if you're interested in laying a solid foundation on this topic.[2]

Within this book, I will focus one hundred percent on the personal, intimate journey into God's presence and communication for each and every person. I am a trained spiritual director and spend most of my days in holy listening as pilgrims traverse their inner landscapes, hungering for connection with God. The chapters that follow are the most common hills and valleys I've witnessed and lived through personally. The relationship between human and divine, between the created and the Creator, is sacred on every level. Every struggle, every fear, every humiliation, every gasp is pivotal. It's meant to lead us somewhere valuable and transformative. And it's all experienced within and through our whole being—spirit, soul, and body. The chapters that follow will discuss the internal complexities we all face as we live in the tension of the now and the not yet, but they will not give you a prescribed roadmap. There isn't one. I've looked.

I invite you to read this book slowly, giving yourself lots of space for self-reflection.[3] What I have learned about the Holy Spirit so far is

---

2   For more information on the Reframing the Prophetic course, please visit www.reframingtheprophetic.com.

3   If you are just beginning on this journey to hear God's voice, it may be good to pair this reading with Pete Greig's book, *How to Hear God: A Simple Guide for Normal People*, where Pete offers a healthy biblical framework from a variety of angles.

that He takes great joy in revealing new rooms within our souls, ones that we didn't know existed. Then, He patiently waits for our invitation to enter. And herein lies the journey.

Chapter 1

The Shallow End

*"Deep calls unto deep
at the sound of your waterfalls."*
Psalm 42:7

Every parent, babysitter, aunt, uncle, or friend of little ones who has ever taken them to a public pool will experience a soulful sigh when I say that the loudest part of every swimming pool is the shallow end. I don't know what it is about this shallow water that seems to amplify every toddler's squeal. I'm sure there's a scientific explanation that could tell me why my ears would ring for hours afterward. But my wonderings were most often drawn to deeper analogies. Just take a quick glance around any sub-culture, and you will find that the loudest part of any people group is the shallow end. The loudest part of any workplace is the shallowness of gossip, slander, back-biting, and petty divisions. The noisiest part of our churches are the disgruntled complainers who care more about how the chairs are arranged than the transformation of people's souls. Somehow, the people who are offended because so-and-so was not asked to cook the roast for the brunch take up the most significant amount of airspace. I wonder if the same scientific explanation could help us understand why these voices are amplified disproportionately.

The loudest part of our broader culture is found in the shallow end as well, loudly displayed by social media. It has become the platform where the shallow end can rage behind closed doors without facing the honest repercussions of face-to-face conversation.

Where this analogy has taken me in recent years has been within my own soul. The loudest part within *me* is most definitely my shallow end, and it has become my biggest nemesis. The most immature parts of me will indeed take up the most room within my thought life and my emotions if I let them. The toddler within me that screams its wants and perceived needs quickly drowns out the deeper heart cries that are desperate to be felt.

As a young person, I would spend every waking moment of the summer in the swimming pool. In middle school, I would often glide to the deep end, roll over onto my back, and gaze at the sky above. Then, I would begin to sweep the water over me, intentionally sinking, surrendering to the deep. I would joyfully allow myself to sink deeper and deeper until the light above me would begin to fade. All the sounds of the other kids in the pool would dissipate, and I would find myself sitting at the bottom of the deepest part of the pool. In that place, I would experience a moment of something truly holy before the air in my lungs forced me to rush back to the surface.

The contrast between the holy of the deep and the noise in the shallow end is a part of our everyday life. I'm sure it's all needed, and it's all holy, to be fair. But the seasons where I find myself stuck in the shallow end (internally and externally) leave me feeling somewhat frazzled and hopeless, sometimes even accusing God of going silent. But then He gently taps me on the shoulder and reminds me I have a choice. The deep end is always there, beckoning me to paddle back to where my heart yearns—if only I would pay attention.

Once or twice a year, I plan a week or two away on a solitude prayer retreat. I am writing this during one of these retreats, sitting on the front porch of a beautiful mountain cabin, warm coffee on the table next to me, gazing at the majesty of a mountainous view. These retreats have been crucial to my spiritual rhythm for many years. Each retreat is dramatically different, but the rhythm is similar. The first day is often filled with the many voices of my own shallow end. Sometimes, it's the toddler, as I previously mentioned. This time around, it's the insecure teenager within me who is causing me the most trouble. As I sat down to turn my full attention to God, I became aware of the anxiety that was vibrating just beneath the surface. "What's that about?" I wondered aloud. The anxiety was all too eager to begin explaining itself, so I listened.

I saw myself at an eighth-grade school dance staring at a boy expressing his desire to dance with me. But for some odd reason, I was more convinced of my unworthiness than of his invitation. My insecurity and shyness were so fierce that I rejected that boy, convinced he didn't want to really dance with me. When, now in my late 50s, I look back on those moments, I wish I could tell my younger self to fling off those lies and stand confidently inside of my own skin, with literal warts and all. *Don't you see this boy's adoration? Receive it! Open your heart to be loved and kick that self-protection instinct in the proverbial behind.* As I lean into this memory, it doesn't take long for me to see the correlation.

Here I sit, eyes wide in wonder at the majesty before me, and I'm reckoning with this instinct yet again. Only this time, it is God who is the one offering the invitation. Why is my instinct of protecting myself rearing its ugly head? Do I fear rejection from God? Is some deep place inside of me feeling unworthy? Where does that come from? My theology tells me I'm always welcome in the presence of God, but my emotions don't always agree with my theology.

When it comes to meeting with God, our whole being matters. Every part of us is invited to this dance, not just the trusting, open-hearted, confidently vulnerable part. If the most honest thing I can bring to Him is my insecure teenager, then that's what I'll do. So I pause, rest into some self-reflection, and invite God into my inner landscape once again. *Insecure teenager faces God* is how I spend my morning. It also sounds like the name of a bad Christian movie.

I recently took a class about the essence of shame, during which I learned from expert psychologists how to address this challenging emotion when it arises in my spiritual directees.[4] They explained how the purpose of shame is to protect us from rejection, but it's only valid if there's a genuine threat of *actual* rejection. Our need for belonging is so fierce that shame believes it is worse to be rejected than to go without food and water. So it guards us from possible rejection at all costs.

The first thing we need to do in the face of shame is to interview it. It's trying to help us, so we don't need to demonize it. We need to determine whether the shame is responding to a valid threat. As I sit here now, I recognize the root of this insecure teenager as shame, but there's no validity to it whatsoever. I know that God will not reject me. So I give shame its moment in the spotlight, listen to its concerns, and

---

4   National Institute for the Clinical Application of Behavioral Medicine, "How to Work With Shame," *NICABM.com*, https://www.nicabm.com/program/shame/?itl=store.

say, "Thank you for trying to protect me, but there's no threat here. I am safe in all of my weaknesses, in all of my failures and broken bits. The whole of me is completely safe in the presence of my Creator."

As I speak these things out loud, giving myself the same mercy and compassion I offer to others, I feel my soul begin to come out of hiding. The voice of the shallow end is quieted, and I can start to glide toward the deep end. Unfortunately, I know that this meeting with my insecure teenager is not finished. It's usually not that easy. I will spend the rest of my day circling back and inviting the Lord to reveal what needs to be seen and understood more deeply. I will intentionally stand before God as openly and vulnerably as possible, parading my raw, unprotected self before Him and receiving His reassurance that I am fully seen, known, and loved. I allowed the loudest part of my internal noise to become an invitation to deep waters with God. Walking this through allowed His voice to open up to me in new ways.

Some of my favorite teachers and authors are Thomas Merton, Robert Mulholland, and Ruth Haley Barton. All three are known for their teachings on the true and false selves. Much of their writing has blessed me thoroughly. I have witnessed, however, people relating to these teachings in a very linear, black-and-white way. These authors do a beautiful job of navigating the nuanced conversations regarding our pretenses, ego masking, and crafting erroneous identities. Yet somehow, it's still tempting for us to take the conversation of the true self versus the false self and flatten it into something altogether unhelpful. We are complex human beings. If we create masks to self-protect or cope in various seasons, then I'm grateful for these survival skills. I think we need to give honor and dignity to these coping mechanisms and thank them for their efforts.

I've personally experienced the kindness of God walking me through laying down defense mechanisms when they were no longer serving me. He sees the *why* behind these emotional management impulses, and it does not dissuade God nor hinder His intimate approach. Yet, the invitation that always stands before us is an ever-increasing journey toward self-awareness. As we grow in awareness of the internal workings within our soul, we learn to open ourselves to experience the presence of God in ever-deepening ways. As David Benner says,

> *"Prayer is what God does in us. Our part has much more to do with consent than initiative. That consent, as we shall see, is simply saying yes to God's invitation to a loving encounter."*[5]

Our willingness to take a compassionate, non-judgmental look within ourselves is a helpful step of learning to hear Him or perceiving His presence. The next step is usually consent, which means learning how to stand before God and open your heart. I am stunned by how easy those three words—"open your heart"—are to say, but how complex their meaning actually is. For many of us, we are so disconnected from our own heart that we don't know what this means. For some, an "open mind" would be easier to comprehend because it relates to being willing to *think* about certain ideas.

But when we talk about opening our heart, we step into a whole different arena. An open heart has more to do with being emotionally available for others. Being someone others find easy to connect with means that your heart is accessible and, therefore, somehow visible. If the thought of this sends a shudder down your spine, you may be someone not naturally at home with vulnerability. It is, indeed, a personality thing.

---

5   David Benner, *Opening to God: Lectio Divina and Life as Prayer* (InterVarsity Press, Kindle Edition), 16.

Some would describe an open heart as a state of being in which you are willing to accept and embrace the experiences and emotions that life brings your way without putting up barriers or defenses. But this is a bit reductionist. Barriers and defenses are a natural part of the human experience. I would prefer to say that we can learn to notice our defenses when they appear and then willingly take them down, choosing to open our hearts again and again.

Emotional openness, humility, and authenticity are closely related, which is an important thread in the true self conversation. Why does this matter in the grand scheme of discerning God's voice, presence, and nearness? On one hand, that's simple to answer. All true intimacy (whether with a spouse, a friend, or God) means that your deepest, most raw, real, authentic self is accessible, touchable, and willing to be influenced. True, deep intimacy gives another the power to affect you deeply, have an impact on you, and see and touch your most authentic self. The less simple reality in this conversation is that this journey will take a lifetime, but it is the essence of all deep, spiritual formation.

Discerning God, hearing His voice, and growing in intimacy with Him will take you down roads of terrifying vulnerability. This world doesn't offer many safe places for this level of knowing and being known. In fact, almost everything in this world rages against such openness. Yet, when it comes to prayer, we must acknowledge that our desperate hunger is to know and be known, to see and be seen, to hear and be heard. So, learning how to open our hearts in an ever-deepening measure is crucial.

Convincing our soul that God is indeed a safe place to bring our whole self is the rugged terrain of faith. Whether it be well-earned trust issues, betrayals, or serious trauma, the life we live on this earth is not an easy one. We journey many painful roads and take on bruises, judgments, vows, etc., some conscious and some unconscious. Learning to trust often defines our spiritual journey. It's profoundly personal, necessarily intimate, and intentionally challenging.

Regardless of our personal history, God stands in front of us—a little like that boy in the eighth grade—with adoration in His eyes, inviting us to a dance. Will we believe that His desire is for us? Will we trust His heart to hold us? Will we lay down our instincts to self-protect, hide, or strive? Flinging our unguarded hearts out in the open before God is one of the most courageous acts of prayer we'll ever do. Our personal, very unique journey will inevitably lead us to this decision, one way or the other.

There are many choices to make along the way, and they're all valid. Whether we say yes to God or walk in the other direction, the invitation remains. You'll most likely make both of these decisions quite often, and it's all okay. Learning to open your heart, regardless of how long it takes, is a holy process. There are many forces that pull us back to the shallow end of the pool. But the deep end is always there, always beckoning, always inviting.

Practice

1. Find a quiet space, sit comfortably, and close your eyes. Spend a few minutes focusing your attention on your thoughts. Immerse yourself in your thoughts without judging or trying to change them. Allow all of your focus to sit within your head and simply observe. Take note of how it feels to be in your head.

2. Open your eyes and jot down a quick bullet point list of the raw thoughts that surfaced. This list is meant for your eyes only, so there's no need to explain anything.

3. Close your eyes once more and shift your focus to your heart. Tune into your emotions and allow yourself to sit with them without judgment or the need to change them. Take a minute to honor the emotions you listed, and gently say, "I see you." Practice opening your heart before God.

4. When ready, open your eyes and write down the emotions you experienced. Name each emotion without further explanation. Acknowledge and honor them by gently saying, "I see you."

5.   Close your eyes again and imagine sitting in front of God with a container in between you. Using your imagination, gently place the raw data of your mind and emotions into the container to be held in safe keeping.

6.   Lastly, close your eyes and redirect your attention to your innermost being, dropping down deeply into your gut. Visualize yourself moving away from the shallow end of a pool and floating into deeper waters. Allow yourself to let go and sink deeper into rest and surrender. Turn your attention toward the internal presence of the Holy Spirit. If it feels right, say His name as you lean into His love, dropping more deeply into quietness and rest.

Reflection Questions

1.   Are you merciful and compassionate toward your internal struggles? If not, why?

2.   What is your relationship with vulnerability? Where are you at peace with vulnerability and where are you resistant? Why?

3.   What is your experience with opening or closing your heart?

4.   To what degree do you feel that your thoughts and emotions crowd your ability to perceive God?

Chapter 2
God Started It

"In the beginning, God..."
Genesis 1:1

Conversation. We usually use this word to refer to a back-and-forth dialogue. Lately, I find myself thinking about nearly all of life as a conversation. In a way, my husband and I have been in a single conversation for 33 years now, including way more than just words. Our emotions and intentions toward each other converse regularly without the use of any words. This ongoing conversation communicates more than our talks over dinner ever have. Words are important, though. And much needed.

But think of all the back and forth that is happening outside of the boundaries of words. All that is sensed, felt, and perceived between people, within atmospheres, and even with nature is a bit like a conversation. Don't worry—I'm not referring to trees talking back to you. But we do have an exchange with nature, don't we? Trees exhale, and we inhale. Flowers display their beauty, giving their fragrance to all who wander past. In return, we squeal in delight and give them our CO_2. The birds dance over our heads as if they're inviting us to join them, and just for a moment, we sense what it may feel like to fly.

As we walk through an art gallery, we connect to something the artist is saying and allow it to have an impact on our inner selves. We may even purchase their piece and empower them to keep creating. As we listen to music, we sing along with the words, move to the rhythm, and allow our hearts to feel the message. There is a back and forth to all of life, a giving and receiving, a sensory exchange, and one could even say—a conversation.

Here in the West, we are living in the most individualistic culture that has walked this earth. It's hard for us to think outside of our little lives. Indigenous American cultures, however, would see themselves as a small part of the whole story of humanity. They would more easily discuss the non-verbal conversation God has had with humanity from the beginning of creation. They recognize that our individual lives are a part of this conversation, but those lives do not stand alone. God began a conversation with humanity at the very beginning, and that conversation has never ceased. I'm not, of course, saying that He's up there rambling and we just need to learn how to snag His words with a proverbial fishing rod. But He is, indeed, communicating and is always inviting us to join in.

One of our many human challenges is that we easily slip into the illusion that there is distance between us and God. We are here, God is way over there, and now we have to find our way to Him. This mindset is replete in much of our language, in many of our worship songs, within our teachings, and in our prayers. Oh, I get it. Our emotional experience of God often feels distant, and it's valuable to put language to this sometimes. But I often wonder if we're setting our subconscious on the wrong foot when this language is more commonplace than it should be. We believe in the omnipresence of God. We memorize Bible verses, such as, "Where can I go from your Spirit? Where can I flee from your presence?" (Psalm 139:7 NIV). Jesus says things like, "When I am raised to life again, you will know that I am in my Father, and you are in me, and I am in you" (John 14:20 NLT).

God is closer to us than we are to ourselves. We say these things, and we know they're true. We know verses that say we "live and move and have our being" in God (Acts 17:28 ESV). But we forget. We live life distracted and emotionally detached from the omnipresence of God. But God isn't distracted, and He's certainly not emotionally detached. He is always present, always near, and always communicating one way or the other. His ways of expressing Himself without words are everywhere, much like my husband's presence conveys so much without a single word spoken.

This may begin to prick at our motive in wanting to hear God's voice. If we are desperate to hear Him only because we need to know if we should take this job, date this person, or move to this city, then our desire is more rooted in transaction than intimate relationship. Of course, it's not bad to want to hear Him before making big decisions. In fact, I would encourage it. But if our entire motive for hearing Him is rooted in a utilitarian approach to living a good life, double-checking our perspective may be good. If we're not careful, we can objectify God for our own purposes.

We all have a mixture of many motives rolling around within our souls at any given moment. Yes, I desire to know God with all my heart. But I also want to make good decisions and remain in God's will. Sometimes, the fear of getting it wrong lurks just beneath the surface.

The ugly truth is that sometimes I just want to be a spiritual guru to impress others. This is the complexity of our humanity, and God sees it all and smiles. Amid our messiness, we are ultimately, profoundly, and consistently loved by God.

We strive. We grasp. We often feel as if it's up to us to position ourselves correctly. We must learn a new skill, spend more time, read more, and do more. If we aren't experiencing fireworks with God, we try to figure out what we've done wrong so that we can fix it. We pray, fast, and try to stir up passion when feeling numb. These are all very normal activities for us primates. It's our way of grasping for control. If we think we can do something different to encounter God, by-golly we're going to figure it out.

But this whole line of thinking is actually unproductive, to say the least. That inner critic tries to convince us that our relationship with God is all on our shoulders. We're simply not that powerful. With this mindset, we train our hearts to believe He's always just out of reach and we must be doing something wrong. There's no winning with the nemesis of control. It's a backstabbing friend at best. It leads us to a striving self-importance that creates pressure for us to perform and fuels a drive for personal achievement. This drive, of course, is only satiated by external validation.

Needless to say, hearing Him or perceiving Him in any real way is going to be very difficult if this is our starting point. Yes, these are things that most people feel and experience, and they're nothing to feel ashamed about. But it's important to recognize these storm clouds for what they are. As Martin Laird, an Augustinian priest and author, beautifully paints a word picture for us, we are the mountain and not the weather. Our true being, our core identity, remains the same, even as the weather patterns of our emotions change. The storm may rage, but the mountain remains stable.[6] You can give yourself permission to disengage with your negative self-talk, naming the root thought patterns as unhelpful or unbiblical, and let the wind blow it away.

God's invitation is to know and be known. To seek to know someone means that we must lay down our personal agenda, open our hearts to receive who they are, and gaze. Learning to be with God in this way will take a lifetime, and this is a gift. It's a marvelous invitation! It helps to remember that pushing aside our agenda is an act of love in and of itself. When we have a plan, timetable, or blueprint for our relationship with God, we are treating Him with disrespect. When we think we can manipulate Him to encounter us a certain way, we presume too much. But when we open our hearts to simply receive Him, in whatever way He desires to be with us, then we are making our soul a hospitable place for the divine.

It's in our original design to connect with God. So, in our deepest, most authentic self, we can't *not* know Him. As St. Augustine says, "Thou hast made us for Thyself, and our hearts are restless until they rest in Thee."[7]

He's always near, always present, and always communicating. He started this conversation, and we're just joining in. When our agendas are put aside and the criticism of our own humanity is quieted, we're free to simply love Him. When we're trying to get something from Him, our heart shifts into striving, and it ceases receiving. When we despise our own neediness or pervert our longing into a defect, we keep ourselves locked inside our self-condemning, striving cage.

When we are just seeking to love Him and know Him, our soul opens in delight. The rest is up to God. How He meets us, if, when, and how He communicates something specifically to us, and whether

---

6   Martin Laird, *Into the Silent Land* (Oxford Univ Press, 2006).
7   Saint Augustine, *Confessions, Book One* (Ignatius Press), chapter one.

He allows us to sense His presence physically are all up to Him. The part that's up to us is our attention and our love.

Coupling our attention with love is the essence of all worship. When we turn our attention toward God, open our heart to receive Him, and let love rise up within our soul, we are very close to discovering our purpose for existence.

> *"The good news is that God is ever reaching out in self-revealing love and has no more ceased being Revelation than being Love itself. The prayer conversation always begins with God. It does not begin with us. Prayer is our response to a divine invitation to encounter. The prayer conversation has already begun because God has already reached out, seeking our attention and response. Until we learn to attend to the God who is already present and communicating, our prayers will never be more than the product of our minds and wills. But prayer has the potential to be so much more. It can be the response of our spirit to God's Spirit as we open the totality of our being to the God who resides in our deep center and longs to meet us there."[8]*

You are surrounded by God. You are encased in Divine Love. His essence can be discovered everywhere your senses alight, if your heart is willing to open, surrender, and love.

---

8   David Brenner, *Opening to God: Lectio Divina and Life as Prayer* (InterVarsity Press, Kindle Edition), 20.

Practice

1. Sit in a comfortable position. Use your imagination and picture God speaking and calling the dust of the earth into being. The dust has the voice of God woven within its fibers.

2. Imagine God taking that dust and forming you, molding you, crafting you, creating you with the substance of His voice.

3. Now, imagine God breathing into your lungs and bringing you to life. Take a deep breath. You are surrounded by His presence, His nearness.

4. What would be the first thing you see when you open your eyes? How would it feel to breathe in the breath of life deeply into your whole being?

Reflection Questions

1. When you turn your attention toward God, what emotion rises in your heart? Why?

2. What is your personal ongoing conversation with God these days?

3. Can you lean into the larger conversation God may be having with your city? With your nation? With the Church?

Chapter 3
Listen

*"Listen, listen to me." God pleads, "and eat what is good,
and you will delight in the richest of fare.
Give ear and come to me; listen, that you may live."*
Isaiah 55:2b- 3a

I sat with a woman in her early 40s who had come for spiritual direction. I knew she had recently gone through the loss of her mom and
she was barely holding it together. So I set my heart to listen and listen
with all my might. For the next two hours, she told me the agonizing
story of sickness, hospitals, injustices, and surprising joys all wrapped
up together in this short season of her life… a season that would
change her forever. The words of Maya Angelou rang in my ear. "There
is no greater agony than bearing an untold story inside of you."[9] How

---

9   Arthur Austin Douglas, *928 Maya Angelou Quotes* (UB Tech, 2016), 65.

true it is. This amazing woman needed to tell this story. And I was given the gift of deeply listening to every sigh, every tear, and every word with my full attention.

Another time, another country, another story, I found myself in Jordan as a wave of refugees arrived. They had run for their lives from ISIS and were sitting in this little church with the look of utter shock on their faces. Each story mattered. Each emotion, each horror, each miracle provision all mattered. For the next several hours, I listened. I listened deeply.

You might have experienced the rare gift of being deeply listened to. Sitting with someone who is fully present, with their attention completely on the whole of you, feels a lot like hope. I've heard people describe moments like this as feeling not just heard but truly seen, understood, and, dare I say, loved. Perhaps you've experienced the gift of intensely and wholeheartedly listening to another. If you have, you know the experience is transcendent. It feels as though you're standing on holy ground, watching a bush that is on fire but not being consumed. Out of all the things that feel sacred to me, deeply listening would be on the top of the list.

What is actually happening when we wholeheartedly listen to another? Our eyes are taking in everything about them. We instinctively study their facial expressions knowing that every turn or twitch of their face communicates something vital. Their hand motions are like punctuation marks. We quietly note the way they're holding their body. If their shoulders are slumped over or tensed up to their ears, it conveys. We take it all in. We notice if their eyes dart away or their head tilts when they're trying to find just the right word or if their lip slightly quivers when they hit a particular part of the story.

When you are truly listening to someone, you engage your entire being, inside and out. Your emotions are invested, rising and falling alongside theirs. You allow yourself to feel every tear, every sigh, every giggle. Your physical senses are awake as if you've thrown yourself into this moment without limitation. You're perceiving way more than the words coming out of their mouth. It's the difference between hearing faint music in the elevator while you're checking your phone versus the experience of being utterly transfixed by a master violinist whose every note awakens emotions you didn't know existed. Your senses engage differently in a noisy shopping mall than they do in the hushed reverence of an art gallery.

This kind of listening requires our imagination to be involved. We must have a willingness to throw ourselves into the moment wholeheartedly, ready to experience the soul of another, journeying *with* them as they speak.

The best listeners learn to cultivate open listening in which they are fully receiving the person in front of them. They're not forming opinions or judgments as the other speaks. They're not listening with the intent of drawing instant assumptions and reacting. They're not interrupting with their own opinions, one-upping them with their own story, robbing them of attention. They're alerted to the sacred yet fragile moment, and they create a sense of space and safety for the other to bring their soul out of hiding. As spiritual director Alice Fryling says, "Intentional listening is indistinguishable from love, and love heals."[10]

Can we listen to God in this same way? Absolutely. When we ask, "How do you hear God's voice?" I often wonder if we're asking the wrong question. Maybe we should ask instead, "How can I learn to truly, deeply listen?"

Evelyn Glennie is a two-time Grammy-winning percussionist

10   Alice Fryling, *Seeking God Together* (InterVarsity Press, 2009), 41.

and considered the world's premier full-time solo percussionist.[11] Watching her perform is a site to behold. She's often surrounded by dozens of instruments and noisemakers, artfully creating sounds that don't seem humanly possible, some of which masterfully mimic the sounds we hear in nature.

But when you find out that she's completely deaf, it's hard to make sense of it. She will tell you that her life's purpose is to teach the hearing community how to truly listen. She explains that she has learned how to use her whole body as an echo chamber, focusing her senses on connecting deeply with every unique sound and becoming intimately acquainted with all the varying vibrations. She also explains that because of her deafness, she isn't distracted by her ears. She has learned to listen in a much deeper way. When I heard her say these words, I froze for several minutes, and the prayer that escaped my lips was, "Lord, please teach me how to turn my whole body into an echo chamber for Your voice. Teach me how to truly listen."

The idea of listening to God with all of our bodily senses is not a new idea, but in my experience, it's not often discussed, especially within charismatic/evangelical circles. We have been guilty of overly separating spiritual things from earthly things. Yet the pattern of Scripture teaches the opposite. Our physical bodies have been radically dignified through the incarnation of Christ. If we dismiss the wisdom of our bodies because somehow we've demonized the natural world, then that's a sad state of affairs.

Have we discounted the spirituality of our senses because we can't make logical sense of them? That's a bit ironic, don't you think? It would be like using one of our areas of intelligence to discount and shut down another area of our innate intelligence. If we are doing this,

---

11   To learn more about Evelyn Glennie, you can visit her website at https://www.evelyn. co.uk/.

then we have likely forgotten how God Himself put on a human body, redeeming it forever.

> *"Earth's crammed with heaven,*
> *And every common bush afire with God;*
> *But only he who sees, takes off his shoes,*
> *The rest sit round it and pluck blackberries."*
> —Elizabeth Barrett Browning[12]

Just look at some of the final lessons that Jesus demonstrated for us. During the most revered, historic dinner of all time, our Lord's final night of enjoying His closest companions, He took a bucket and a hand towel and began to wash their feet. He didn't preach to them; instead, He acted, touched their skin, held their feet in His hands, and wiped them tenderly. Through these actions, He spoke more words than could ever be written down. Then He took two very tangible items—bread and wine—and told them to take and eat. *This is My body. Chew. Swallow. Digest Me. Remember Me.* These two physical activities are sacramental moments where heaven and earth collide in bodily form. Why, then, would we assume that our physical bodies are not included in connecting with God?

The notion that our body plays a vital role in listening to God may be a novel concept for many; however, upon reflection, it becomes clear that this connection is an innate aspect of our human experience. I heard one doctor refer to humans as one big sense organ. *All* of our senses are activated when we're listening, whether to others or to God. As one of the early Church fathers, Iranaeus, wrote (as adapted and translated by Scott Cairns):

---

12   Elizabeth Barrett Browning, *Aurora Leigh, Book 7* (Oxford World Classics, 2008), 246.

"The tender flesh itself will be found one day—quite surprisingly—to be capable of receiving, and yes, fully capable of embracing the searing energies of God. Go figure. Fear not. For even at its beginning the humble clay received God's art, whereby one part became the eye, another the ear, and yet another this impetuous hand. Therefore, the flesh is not to be excluded from the wisdom and the power that now and ever animates all things. His life-giving agency is made perfect, we are told, in weakness— made perfect in the flesh."[13]

Many of us have ignored our body's role in listening. Our senses may feel as if they have fallen asleep and could use a little nurturing. There are many ways to awaken our senses, but mostly, we are to give them their due attention. We have been created in a most miraculous way. So we should spend some time each day listening to God with our bodies and remembering that it's more natural for our senses to perceive God than it is for us to drink water. The Holy Spirit wants to awaken us, stir us, and train us in this kind of listening. He's on our side. He understands how forgetful we are. Maybe this is why He gave us something to do with our bodies, taking His communion into our innermost being to help us remember.

Countless influential philosophers, mystics, artists, and theologians throughout history have taught us the interconnectedness of the natural and the supernatural. They've come to understand that everything we see and everything that is created serves as a sign and a symbol for a deeper, unseen truth. This perspective fundamentally alters how we engage with the world, fostering a sacramental worldview that perceives everything as sacred due to its intrinsic connection to God.

---

13   St. Irenaeus (c. 125–c. 210), adapted and translated by Scott Cairns.

In times past, this mode of thought was more widespread, but it has gradually diminished within some of our modern day expressions of Christianity. As a result, our relationship with our bodies and the rest of creation has become more secular than sacred.

The essence of the sacramental worldview lies in recognizing that nothing in creation is merely mundane or ordinary. Every aspect of life, from the dirt beneath our feet to the seeds of cottonwood trees, reveals something profound about Christ. God's presence is not detached from creation but is intimately woven into the fabric of our world. Everything in the universe—every star, every tree, every body—proclaims some truth about its maker, and therefore preaches the Gospel of Jesus Christ.

God did not create His creation as an everlasting witness to Himself and then withdraw from it. Rather, He is intimately woven through it. The sacramental worldview helps us see that. It shows us that heaven and earth aren't separated from each other, and they aren't asking us to figure out how to bridge the gap.

Heaven and earth have kissed over and over again. It's our awareness of that kiss that we can learn to cultivate. One of the most important aspects of this cultivation is the prayer of silence, and the most important aspect of the prayer of silence is attention. I can be silent for hours but not give any attention to the Lord. My attention seems to be what everyone and everything is fighting for. Whether it be social media algorithms, billboards littering the countryside trying to sell their wares, or the preacher on the stage who is passionately trying to hold my attention. It is clearly a very valuable commodity.

The French philosopher Simone Weil says, "Attention is the rarest and purest form of generosity,"[14] and I find this to be deeply true. Our attention spans have quietly suffered the consequences of

---

14   Simone Weil, *Simone Weil: A Life* (Haus Publishing, reprint edition 2018).

our digital age, much like a forest that has been mowed down when no one was watching for the sake of catalogs. All these important aspects of our humanity have suffered immense fragmentation.

Our overstimulated brains have become addicted to dopamine-flooded distractions, and we have paid a high price. Without redeeming our attention spans, we risk losing many cherished gifts. But the biggest of these losses, in my opinion, is our ability to listen deeply for any length of time. We can grieve this loss, rightfully so. But we can also change. Small changes in our daily activities, like taking intentional blocks of time without screens, notifications, social media, etc., can begin to increase our attention span in dramatic ways.

Sit outside, listen for the birds, pay attention to the wind blowing through the trees. Remind yourself that you are drenched in the presence of our omnipresent God. Pay attention to the holy that surrounds you. Listen for *Him*, not just His words. Turn your awareness to His ongoing conversation, and make your soul a hospitable place for His love. Do this every day, for longer and longer periods of time, and your attention span will begin to strengthen.

If you want to get serious about raising your attention span from the dead, then engage in a fast from all screens for eight days. When we unplug, it takes our mind about eight days to fully calm down and rest.[15] It's a muscle that may be atrophied, but it's still there and can, indeed, be revived.

"The state of our attention determines the state of our lives."[16]

Strengthening your attention span will help you awaken your

---

15   Daniel Levitin, "Hit the Reset Button in Your Brain," *NYTimes.com*, August 9, 2014, https://www.nytimes.com/2014/08/10/opinion/sunday/hit-the-reset-button-in-your-brain.html.

16   Chris Bailey, "How to Get Your Brain to Focus," *YouTube.com*, April 5, 2019, 15:15, https://www.youtube.com/watch?v=Hu4Yvq-g7_Y.

senses. Our senses are funny like that. They just want to be acknowledged. It's like they're waiting for their moment in the spotlight ready to show off. As you read this sentence, I encourage you to pause, close your eyes, and see if you can feel the air on your skin. If you're outside and you have the pleasure of a slight breeze, this will be easy. But if you're inside, know that the air is just as present when it's not moving. It's still resting on your skin. You're breathing it in. You may not be aware of it throughout most of your day, but it's keeping you alive.

It's a bit like this with God's presence. We are easily aware of Him when the wind is blowing, but the longing of our hearts points us to an increasing awareness of His constant nearness. Awakening our senses to perceive His presence in the stillness is a holy act of remembrance. Imagine yourself deeply listening to your best friend and being present with God in the same way. Rest in the knowledge of His nearness, whether you feel anything tangible or not. Turn your awareness to God's omnipresence throughout your day and simply appreciate Him. Listen to His nearness. Listen to His presence in the world. Practice listening to God with your whole body and see what awakens inside of you.

Practice

1. Let go of your striving, your agenda. If it helps to communicate your needs to the Lord, then do so first, and then release.

2. Allow your heart to fill with love and peace. Choose an attitude of joy and contentment just to be *with* God.

3. Say hello.

4. Know that He is near.

5. Receive joyfully what He wants to do, say, or not say.

6. Simply love His presence, regardless of what you feel.

Reflection Questions

1. What is your relationship with your body? Do you listen to your body? How do you treat your body?

2. What do you think about your body being an abiding place for the Holy Spirit? Would God speak to you through your body?

3. How does your heart listen?

Chapter 4

A Meditation

"This is how you pray continually, not by offering prayer in words, but by joining yourself to God through your whole way of life, so that your life becomes one continuous and uninterrupted prayer."[17]
—St. Basil the Great

The substance of God's voice is altogether experiential.

Let's begin with a couple of simple yet profound thoughts. The Lord of all Creation has chosen you as His dwelling place. He is within you. When He speaks, you can sometimes feel it in the core of your being. Other times you can sense His voice moving through you like

---

17   St. Basil the Great, "Take Heed, Watch and Pray," *UKMidCopts.org*, July 2016, https://ukmidcopts.org/resources/contemplations/take-heed-watch-and-pray-for-you-do-not-know-when-the-time-is-mark-1333-this-is-how-you-pray-continually-not-by-offering-prayer-in-words-but-by-joining-yourself-to-god-through-y/#.

a soft current. You can learn to become more conscious of His voice rumbling within your soul. But learning to recognize His voice is not a work, nor is it something that striving can attain. It is found within love, and love is expressed in surrender.

So today, simply love His voice. Don't work to hear it. Don't labor to achieve it. Don't toil to understand it. Just surrender and love His voice. Love listening to Him. Love sensing Him. Allow your heart to simply love relating to Him.

Giving our hearts to this love affair positions us to be more deeply rooted in rest and grace, propelling us down a road of freedom, intimacy, and encounter with God. Go deeper still. Let your heart gaze upon the One who made you, and tell Him how you love perceiving Him, sensing Him, and knowing Him. It often feels like a dance. We step with God in musical harmony. He speaks, we believe. He nudges, we act. He smiles, we grow. He corrects, we learn. This all happens within the embrace of the dance. The dance of grace. The dance of mystery. The dance of joy. Dancing our way through life, enthralled with the sound of His being. Jesus Christ, our Lord and our King. He's absolutely enchanting.

Chapter 5
With

Things break. Our hearts break. We break.
But waves also break. So does bread. As does the day.
We break into laughter, break through barriers,
and break new ground.
Maybe it's not the breaking that's hard –
but what comes before.
And maybe, just maybe,
what comes after the breaking
is hope.

My Dark Night Journey

I thought I had a robust theology about suffering. I've never been one of those who thought God was just there to make my life more enjoyable. I scoffed quietly at the genie-in-the-bottle belief systems that led people to believe they were safe from all trials and could expect health, wealth, and prosperity from the God of the Bible. Yet, when my grandbaby was born desperately ill and the doctors told us to prepare for the worst, my emotions told a different story. I walked the streets for endless hours, crying and yelling at God, begging and pleading. I even threatened God with a thing or two without any care for theological correctness. I remember hearing the words, "Don't you dare," come out of my lips in between sobs. I knew what I was doing when I was doing it, which made it worse. All of my robust theology flew out the window. I watched it go and didn't care. Pain won. Fear won—at least for a few days.

A few months later, my 28-year-old son was rushed to the hospital on the brink of death. A sudden onset of Type One diabetes was the violent perpetrator. He was in full-blown kidney failure, and his body was shutting down rapidly. The medical staff spent several hours trying to get access to a vein in his pale, dehydrated body. The next unbearable hours were a fight for his life. I stayed silent this time around. No begging, pleading, or bargaining. Not a single threat came out of my lips. But not a single prayer was spoken either. I was terrified and silent.

When life jolts you, assaults you, or terrifies you, your heart will indeed react.

It can't help but react. Suffering will expose every dark and dusty corner of your soul. I could take the rest of this chapter to lay out a solid, healthy, biblical understanding of suffering. I could try to defend myself for why my theology didn't hold up when it was tested. But instead, I'd prefer to talk about God's response to our pain, regardless of what horrid belief system leaks through the cracks.

In the months that followed, I put a wall up between God and me, and it was a thick one. Once again, I knew I was doing it. I didn't want to, and I knew it was a pain reaction that was unhelpful. I could hear the words I would have told one of my spiritual directees if they were doing what I was doing. But my logic didn't seem to be in charge of this one. My heart was leading the way, and I felt powerless to stop it.

My grandson and son are both alive and well today, yet my faith took a beating through the trauma of it all. I felt quite ashamed, if I'm honest. I have friends who have lost children and grandchildren, and their faith seemed amazingly strong and steady from the looks of things. Yet, here I was. Not only did I feel helpless day after day as I sat facing this wall that I had erected between me and God, but now I was judging myself because of it.

Our journey through trial and suffering is varied, of course. I wouldn't expect yours to be the same as mine. But I wonder if certain twisted pathways are more common than we realize. We may instinctively recoil from a God who feels unsafe. When we feel our world is falling apart, we may indeed wall up and hide, trying desperately to create a safe distance from the God whose character is suddenly and surprisingly in question. Is He good? Our indoctrinated brain may confidently say, *Of course! Don't you remember all those sermons you heard about the goodness of God?* But our hearts are not so easily convinced, especially when life screams.

For the three years before these near-death traumas in my family, I was in a very difficult place spiritually. It felt as though God was getting more and more distant as the world became more and more ablaze. These were the years of the global pandemic. Covid was a big domino that toppled my nation into chaos. At a time when people were reaching out to me regularly to hear what I thought God was saying, I felt as though He had just disappeared. I had been through dry, desert seasons before, but this felt like something different. There was a large empty void within me that I was powerless to alter. I couldn't sense Him, perceive Him, and I certainly wasn't hearing anything from Him.

A part of me silently wondered if I had done something terribly wrong and God was mad at me. I wrestled with feelings of rejection and abandonment. I would preach the Gospel to my soul and feel no solace. I could give myself all the "right" answers, but that didn't stop my emotions from hopping on multiple runaway trains every single day. I wondered where I had gotten off track and why God had seemingly left me. The wrestle between my heart and my head had never been quite this fierce.

This could be why my heart responded with fists up, ready for a fight when my grandbaby nearly died. My sense of connection with God was already strained from this emotional roller coaster. My heart was frazzled, to say the least. Through the help of my spiritual director and some wise counselors, I eventually began to chip away at the wall of self-protection I had carefully constructed. But the felt sense of His nearness didn't return for quite some time.

My season has shifted, and I'm thankful; however, this particular dark night will be one that I will be unpacking for a long time to come.

Why am I telling you all of this? Because it feels important to include the whole, big, messy human story when we talk about our relationship with God's voice. The ups and downs and the tragic, squirrely places our hearts wander sometimes, *must* be talked about because it all *must* be experienced. I can already tell you that these years of the dark night of my soul are some of the most valuable years of my life. I learned more about God in His perceived absence than I could possibly write in this book. When my faith was nearly smashed to pieces, God held the crumbs. My powerlessness confronted me every single day.

Yet, deep inside, I knew God wouldn't budge. He would not let go. Would I dare to believe that His presence was still surrounding me when I couldn't feel a thing? Could I still trust His omnipresence when parts of me were doubting His existence? Somehow, through the absence of any felt sense of His nearness, I knew He was still there. It was His patience that dumbfounded me. I knew He was waiting. Patiently, lovingly waiting.

Many of the most influential mystics, contemplatives, and philosophers who have written on spiritual formation will share similar stories of going through long seasons of life where they experienced the absence of God's felt presence. It's important to know that this experience is normal. It could be caused by our emotions retracting in fear or trauma that gets a hold of us. Or it may just be a journey God has, in His wisdom, carved out for us. Regardless, we must know that seasons like this are vital for maturing our soul and deepening our spiritual journey. They aren't a hiccup in the journey. They're not a stumbling block, a problem that needs to be fixed, or a detour from the path. They *are* the path. At least part of the path.

During these years, I was aware that my heart felt unsafe, and no matter what theological gymnastics I performed, I learned that there was no rushing this process. I didn't choose it, at least I didn't *think* I chose it. Yet, this is where I found myself. I didn't want to be on this particular path, that much I knew, but there was no way out. During the first few treacherous miles, all I wanted to do was find a different way. I was looking for the exit signs, desperately wanting to work my way out of this maze. Eventually, I embraced the truth that I was not in charge of this (whatever "this" was), and I simply gave in to it.

All I could do was surrender to the hand of God, even though I knew my heart didn't feel safe. I felt as if He and I were locked in a room, staring each other down, and He had won. I fell into the chair, exasperated, and said, "Do what You must." I had to admit that He was *with* me, even though it didn't feel like it. He was doing something, even though it felt as if He had left me. He may not have been speaking or leading me in any tangible way, but somehow He was, in fact, still *with* me.

Emmanuel

If someone who had never heard of the God of the Jews, the person of Jesus, or had any knowledge of Christianity stumbled across the Bible and read it cover to cover, it's likely they would understand it as a story of a majestic, all-powerful Creator who is unseeable but not unknowable. In fact, this unseeable God seems to be going to great lengths to be with His people.

The beginning of the story starts with God breathing life into His creation. Can you imagine Adam opening his eyes for the first time? What did he see? Would he have been looking directly into the face of God who had just performed mouth-to-mouth? Just a few days later, there were two humans in the Garden, and God was walking with them in the cool of the day. With-ness begins.

Later in the story, as the Israelites wandered through the wilderness, the Lord spoke to Moses and asked him to build a tabernacle so that He could dwell amongst His people. Let's think this through. He's God. He's everywhere. He is already present and speaks with Moses regularly. He is guiding them in tangible and powerful ways. And yet, it seems He wants a house in the neighborhood.

About twelve generations later, the construction of Solomon's temple begins. God still wanted a house. He wanted to live in the neighborhood permanently. We can read about the inauguration of the first temple in 2 Chronicles 7:1-5. When Solomon finished praying, fire came down from heaven, and the glory of the Lord filled the temple so strongly that the priests could not enter. Over 100,000 people saw the visible infilling on the day God moved into the house they had built. Once again, the with-ness of God is clear. The temple became the center of Jewish culture for obvious reasons. If you had Yahweh living in the house down the street, I think your life would revolve around that house as well. It was the holiest place on earth. It was sacred in every conceivable way—even in ways that we don't understand. They saw the temple as the connection point between heaven and earth, and it was. The meeting place between God and man. All so that *God could be* with *them*.

Think about Mary. She was an unmarried, Jewish teenager. She receives an uninvited visit from the angel Gabriel who fills her room with his radiance and gives Mary her instructions.

"Do not be afraid, Mary; you have found favor with God. You will conceive and give birth to a son, and you are to call him Jesus. He will be great and will be called the Son of the Most High. The Lord God will give him the throne of his father David, and he will reign over Jacob's descendants forever; his kingdom will never end.[18]"

Mary trembles, but she stays present. And then she says yes. "*Hineni*. Here I am. Your will be done." And the angel answered her, "The Holy Spirit will come upon you, and the power of the Most High will overshadow you; therefore the child to be born will be called holy—the Son of God" (Luke 1:35 ESV).

This scene is a bit like the infilling of Solomon's temple. There's a move-in day where God's tangible presence will abide on the earth, but instead of announcing His presence before 100,000 people, He chose the hiddenness of a womb. The intimacy between God and this young girl is astonishing. There's no way around the picture that is

18   Luke 1:30-33 NIV

being drawn here. Yes, it's a reflection of the inauguration of Solomon's temple. But it is also a reflection of profound intimacy.

It wasn't enough for Him to be in a building made with hands where people could come and visit. He put on flesh and bone and walked among us. This time, He chose to entrust Himself to a woman's body.

The placenta that held Him within her is built of cells from both the mother and the baby, serving as a conduit for the exchange of life and growth for nine months. As early as the second week of pregnancy, there is a two-way flow of cells and DNA between the baby and the mother. Cells containing DNA from the baby cross the placenta and enter the mother's blood circulation, while cells from the mother cross in the opposite direction and transfer into the baby's circulation.

Tertullian, one of the greatest and most well-known early Church fathers, says, "Pray, tell me, why the Spirit of God descended into a woman's womb at all if He did not do so for the purpose of partaking of flesh from the womb. For He could have become spiritual flesh without such a process—much more simply, indeed, outside of the womb than in it. He had no reason for enclosing Himself within one if He was to bear forth nothing from it."[19]

"Jesus is made 'of her,' not just 'in her.' He is made from her and not just through her. She is not only a receptacle of the Divine; she contributes from her own body. It is her blood that forms him, her food that nourishes him."[20]

For nine months, she walked the earth carrying the divine within her. Every minute, every hour, every day. She walked the earth carrying the holy and majestic One within her body. Her cells weaving

---

19   Tertullian, "On the Flesh of Christ," *EarlyChristianWritings.com*, 2024, http://www.earlychristianwritings.com/text/tertullian15.html#google_vignette.
20   Lucy Peppiatt, "On God's Mother, *WTCTheology.org.uk*, December 2013, https://wtc-theology.org.uk/theomisc/on-gods-mother-lucy-peppiatt/#:~:text=Jesus%20is%20made%20'of%20her,her%20breasts%20that%20feed%20him.

with His, her DNA knitting itself together with His. Some saw the sign. Most did not. Her life was the beginning of a new reality, a new humanity. This is prophetic at its core. An echo of what was to come.

Mary has been called the third temple. She's also been called the new Ark of the Covenant. Her young, innocent body was carrying the living presence of God on the earth. Her *body*. Not just her spirit. Not within her gifting, her ministry, or her charisma.

As we know, Jesus referred to Himself as the temple. It's mind-blowing and more than just a little scandalous to think that the temple would now be within human flesh. Holiness intermingled with a woman's body, carrying the physical embodiment of the meeting place of heaven and earth.

With-ness exemplified.

Now, let's talk about Jesus. God incarnate walked the earth amongst His people. In John 2, right after He ran through the temple flipping over the tables, He announced that He is the temple. This was shocking enough. But then, He died. For a terrifying three days, the world held its breath. The empty tomb, the curtain of the holy of holies torn in two. Over the next forty days, His resurrected body walked amongst humanity. The Creator conquered death and visited His creation over and over again until it was time to ascend.

"When the day of Pentecost arrived, they were all together in one place. And suddenly there came from heaven a sound like a mighty rushing wind, and it filled the entire house where they were sitting. And divided tongues as of fire appeared to them and rested on each one of them. And they were all filled with the Holy Spirit and began to speak in other tongues as the Spirit gave them utterance" (Acts 2:1-6 ESV).

This, my friends, is another move-in day. This time, however, it's with us, the community of believers. The tongues of fire symbolized the fire on the altar that was to burn continually. It represented the dwelling place of God.

The holy of holies has moved location. This is not only unfathomable, but it's scandalous on every level. We are now the dwelling place of God. He has taken His with-ness to a level that the holy is now intertwined with fragile humanity. His desire to be with is now *within*.

THIS IS EMMANUEL.

Looking back on this dark night of the soul, I can say it broke me open in ways I never expected. It revealed a deeper truth I couldn't have learned any other way. My tidy theology didn't hold—my emotions took the lead, and I wrestled long and hard with silence, fear, and the absence of God's felt presence. I didn't realize I had become overly confident in hearing His voice a certain way. That limitation hindered my journey toward deeper intimacy. In the stillness and the ache, I discovered Emmanuel. He was revealing Himself to me *within* the absence. I didn't need to do anything to get back to Him; He had never left. His unwavering presence through my wavering faith has become the anchor of my soul. My experience of God has shifted dramatically since these years, and I'm eternally grateful. I can now look back and see the sacred path where with-ness became my reality.

Practice

Read the following poem slowly, contemplating each point deeply, pausing often to allow the truth of these words to sink deeply into your soul.

> *His patience is unfathomable.*
> *His commitment is unshakable.*
> *He is always.*
> *Habitually*
> *With.*
> *He taps on that flimsy door you tried to shut*
> *Over and over again.*
> *Whispering to your soul.*
> *"It's time to come out of hiding."*
> *And you will discover*
> *Ever so gradually.*
> *That even in the shadows*
> *Of mistrust and fear.*
> *He was speaking.*
> *Even during the battle*
> *Between your body, your mind, and your soul.*

He was echoing
His love.
Reminding you over and over again,
That He is indeed,
Oh so very good.
Today, my friends, I want you to know
That your heart doesn't stop hearing.
Even when it's in hiding,
When your walls think they're protecting,
When your soul runs in the other direction.
Your heart will still hear Him.
Don't worry.
He will wait.

Reflection Questions

1. How often do you think about God's presence dwelling within you?

2. Do you find yourself believing that God is only with you when you're doing all the right spiritual things? Why?

3. Do you instinctively feel as though God is far off and you need to "work" your way to Him in prayer? Why?

Chapter 6
Eyes That See

I remember walking down streets when I was a budding 14-year-old girl and glancing at my reflection in the shop windows as I walked by. Of course, many of us do, just to make sure there isn't toilet paper dragging from our belt or some random piece of newspaper stuck to our bum. But at 14, I remember that odd sensation of truly not knowing what I was going to look like day after day. I was changing so rapidly, morphing into an adult human, and I had no idea how this transformation was going to turn out. Every time I looked in the mirror, I had a mixture of anxiety and excitement. Who was I becoming? Shop windows were irresistible.

One day was especially memorable, because I found myself walking alone on a busy street that was littered with shop windows. Because there was no one else rushing me along, I wandered slowly. I kept trying to sneak glances over my right shoulder to see my reflection while not wanting to appear vain. But the draw to study myself won out. So I stopped walking and stood in front of a store with especially clean windows surveying my reflection with a quizzical eye.

After a few minutes, my eyes shifted to what was inside the shop. The odd looking plastic people in the window caught my attention. They were dressed in outrageous clothing with audacious hats upon their heads. The stuffed dogs at their feet were a bit alienesque. I giggled over the way they were posed and tried to mimic them. I allowed my eyes to shift further into the store, trying to make out what they were selling. I saw more clothing, some fancy white tables with shoes, purses, and jewelry displayed, and people milling about.

There was a mother and daughter shopping together, and I could feel the tension between them. I saw a very tired woman who was walking slowly, pushing a stroller and absent-mindedly letting her fingers graze the tops of the hangers. Her mind was clearly somewhere else altogether. There was a young girl behind the counter picking her fingernails. She looked worried about something, and I wondered what it was. I became totally engulfed in imagining each of their stories, until someone on the sidewalk slammed into me and stumbled onward as if I was a speed bump.

Jolted back to reality, I began walking again, only this time I brought the people in the shop with me. Each store front I walked by, I would glance at myself, look at the display behind the windows, and then try to focus my eyes as deeply inside the window as possible before moving on. This felt like a fun game to pass the time—but it has become one of my biggest life lessons.

When we first meet someone, our first glance is like a stone skipping across the surface of the water. We hardly look at them with any depth at all. But if we pause, we may be able to sense the invitation to look a little deeper. If we engage our heart with intentional kindness mixed with loving curiosity, our eyes will begin to see a little more of their true essence. The more we open our hearts to love, the more our eyes will see.

> *"Now one of the Pharisees was requesting Him to dine with him, and He entered the Pharisee's house and reclined at the table. And there was a woman in the city who was a sinner; and when she learned that He was reclining at the table in the Pharisee's house, she brought an alabaster vial of perfume, and standing behind Him at His feet, weeping, she began to wet His feet with her tears, and kept wiping them with the hair of her head, and kissing His feet and anointing them with the perfume. Now when the Pharisee who had invited Him saw this, he said to himself, 'If this man were a prophet He would know who and what sort of person this woman is who is touching Him, that she is a sinner'"* (Luke 7:36–39 NASB1995).

This woman was not only *not* invited to the Pharisee's home for dinner, she was actually risking her life by entering into this holy man's dwelling. For a sinful woman to enter a home as she did was beyond daring. Who was this woman, and why did she risk her life by plunging into the house of a Pharisee without invitation? My only guess is that she had come to the unwavering belief that Jesus was indeed the Messiah. Why else would she take such a massive risk just to meet Him? Had she been watching Him for several days? Had she fallen in love with this Man who embraced the outcast, defended the broken, and dignified the shamed?

The alabaster vial of perfume was probably her dowry. I'm sure she didn't carry it with her every day, so she must have run home to get it. I think she planned to pour her life savings upon Jesus as a sign of devotion and adoration. But I'm not sure she could've planned the emotion involved. I wonder what she felt as she gave Him her everything? Yes, I think she knew who He really was. Somehow she had put the pieces together and believed He was the Messiah. With this revelation, her actions made sense. If you knew that the Son of God was in the house down the street, you may have done the same.

The part of this story that terrifies me is that all of the others were sitting at the same table utterly clueless of the true identity of their dinner guest. They were eating dinner with the Incarnate One, in the presence of Majesty, but they were blind. This sinful woman could *see* Him accurately and had the only appropriate response. She did what any sane person would've done if they knew they were face-to-face with the Son of God. The others in the room were eating dinner casually, asking for someone to pass the vegetables. This is the true scandal of the story.

I don't know if this woman had spoken with Jesus before, yet these Pharisees were eating a long meal with Him, chatting it up over lamb. What was it about her that could see Him for who He really was? And what was it about the Pharisees that blinded them?

We see this dynamic again in John's writings. Philip, who had been hanging out with Jesus every morning, noon, and night, had just asked Him to reveal God the Father. "Jesus said to him, 'Have I been so long with you, and yet you have not come to know Me, Philip? He who has seen Me has seen the Father'" (John 14:9 NASB1995). These men had seen unimaginable miracles, they had heard Jesus proclaim that He was the Christ, and they had been present when Jesus claimed to be *one* with God. The Pharisees heard Jesus make the same kind of claims, and they tried to stone Him because of it. After all this time, had Philip not yet truly *seen* Him?

Maybe our eyes aren't the key to seeing. We've already talked about how true hearing is a fully embodied experience, which includes the eyes. This much is pretty obvious to most of us. In fact, we could almost say that we hear with our eyes as much as with our ears, right? But what if we're not *truly* seeing? What does it mean to truly see, and how does this correlate to hearing God's voice?

Jacques Lusseyran was a French author and political activist who lived during World War II. At the age of seven, he had an accident that blinded him completely in both eyes. A few days after he lost his sight, this young boy exclaimed that he could see, but not with his eyes. He said that something was illuminating his vision from within, like "'light rising, spreading, resting on objects, giving them form, then leaving them.' He was able to live in this stream of inner light which, like outer light, illuminated objects and people, giving them form and full color."[21] He was considered the blind man who learned how to see by the light of God that dwelt within him. His great revelation was that true light came from within and not from without. Truly astounding.

There are many things about Jacques' story that are remarkable. But I'm most captured by the idea that his eyes were not necessary to see what matters most. In fact, much like Evelyn Glennie, Jacque wondered if functioning eyeballs were actually a hindrance to deep seeing. How does our heart see? How does the internal presence of God illuminate the world around us? What does it mean to truly see beyond the surface of the images our eyeballs capture?

In the Bible, we see the contrast between what humans saw versus what God saw. God tested His prophets in their vision, and He challenged the religious leaders in *how* they saw others. The contrast between what people saw and what God saw was cavernous. People saw Gideon as a coward, but God said he was a mighty warrior. People

21   Jacques Lusseyran, *Against the Pollution of the I* (Novato, California: New World Library, 2006), 11.

saw Abraham and Sarah as barren, but God said Abraham was the father of many nations. People saw Moses as a stuttering, insecure man, but God saw him as a deliverer of nations. People saw Peter as an over zealous hypocrite, but God saw that he was a rock. People saw Zacchaeus as a thief, but God saw him as an honest man.

I've read many books on the subject of seeing, and each one of them has been rather disappointing. That disappointment primarily came because the aim of the book was to teach a certain spiritual skill so that the reader could conquer something, acquire something, or become gifted at some sort of spiritual ability. But I think that goal misses the point entirely.

"Hear this, O foolish and senseless people, who have eyes but see not, who have ears, but hear not" (Jeremiah 5:21 ESV).

"Son of man, you dwell in the midst of a rebellious house, who have eyes to see, but see not, who have ears to hear, but hear not" (Ezekiel 12:2 ESV).

Both of these passages are referring to people who have physical ears and eyes, and yet they are not hearing or seeing what matters most. As we modern-day folks read this indictment, we should take it very seriously. We have the same tendency to see with our eyes, but not really see, and to hear with our ears, but not really hear. The whole world is awash with the glory of God, if only we are looking for it. Our eyes are created to see His glorious presence absolutely everywhere, but we have been trained by a distracted, disconnected culture to look only at the reflection in the store front window.

How often do we look at someone long enough to see past what's immediately visible? I'm not talking about staring weirdly into someone's eyes for long enough to make them wonder about your intentions. What I'm referring to only takes seconds, if we would simply pause and focus our attention past the surface. The first glance is rarely compassionate anyway, so it's worth taking a few extra moments in our day to practice looking a little deeper. This is a spiritual discipline, and it may prove to be more significant in your life with God than anything else you'll ever do. Learning how to look deeply at others without judgment, agenda, or opinion will alter everything about you, changing forever how you walk through this world.

If we can see human beings, and everything God has created for that matter, as His personal expression, we may begin to understand that His glory can truly be seen throughout the whole earth. When you walk through an art gallery, you are hopefully wandering slowly, stopping in front of each masterpiece to gaze and contemplate. If you took an art appreciation course in school, you may have learned to saunter through galleries in a deeper way, *encountering* the art—emotionally, physically, and visually, bringing all of your senses into this most intimate moment. It becomes a conversation between you the art, but a conversation without words. The piece may speak to you deeply, or it may trouble your soul. It may lead you down memory lane, or it may inspire you to think in a new way.

You may wonder about the artist and what moved them to create that piece of art. Through their work, you get a glimpse into who they are, while allowing their creation to have a unique impact on you. Art is the communication of intimate concepts that cannot be faithfully portrayed by words alone. An artist's creation is powerful communication that invites us to look beyond the obvious and engage our entire being with what is unspoken. Isadora Duncan, who was a pioneer of modern contemporary dance said, "If I could tell you what it meant, there would be no point in dancing it."[22]

God is the master artist, as we all know. But we do not often wander through this world with the same posture as we do an art gallery. Maybe this is the invitation. "Our failure is not that we chose earth over heaven: it is that we fail to see the divine in the earth, already active and working, pouring forth grace and spilling glory into our lives."[23]

> *"The heavens declare the glory of God, and the sky above proclaims his handiwork"* (Psalm 19:1 ESV).

> *"The earth is full of the steadfast love of the LORD"* (Psalm 33:5 ESV).

In the Bible, Jesus says, "He who has ears to hear, let him hear" eight times in the Gospels and seven times in the book of Revelation. He often says something like this after He tells the people a story in which there was a message. He didn't speak in linear, black and white, concrete ways. In fact, the prophets in the Old Testament were all considered poets. As they communicated the words of God to the listening world, they did it through poetry, prose, and artistic demonstration. They used artistic ways to communicate, because it requires a deeper engagement from the receiver. Often God would ask them to look at something and tell Him what they saw.

What we see and how we see it seems to matter when it comes to perceiving God's messages. It stands to reason that if we want to learn to hear God's voice, we should learn to listen for poetry, we should

---

22   Isadora Duncan, *My Life* (Liveright Publishing, 1927).
23   Makoto Fujimura, *Silence and Beauty: Hidden Faith Born of Suffering* (Downers Grove, IL, InterVarsity Press, 2016), 118.

open our eyes to see artistic demonstration, and we should learn to see beyond the surface to perceive the voice of the Master Artist. The answer Jesus gave to those struggling with anxiety was, "Look at the birds" (Matthew 6:26 ESV). He didn't encourage them to get therapy (although I do love and recommend a good therapy session). He first told them to look at the birds and study them. Clearly, what we're looking at and what we're truly seeing can speak volumes.

Once again, we're talking about other senses operating at much deeper levels within our internal being. Our heart sees. Our body sees. Our emotions see. Our spirit sees. And I believe they're all connected and integrated, woven together within our humanity. I do not believe it's helpful to discuss "spiritual seeing" as separate from the whole. Healthy spirituality should be integrated within our heart, mind, soul, and body. As we are looking beyond the surface of any situation, we are looking with eyes of love and compassion. We are connected and aware of the presence of the Holy Spirit, and we are seeking to look beyond what the eye can see.

Each human being is an artful expression of God's love. Every tree, leaf, insect, mountain, river, amoeba, and animal is an expression of its Maker. Eyes of love can see it. Love causes us to look beneath the surface to see the essence of the Creator's expression. Love sees. Our connection with the love of God will tune our vision to a whole different channel. Love opens the awareness that there's more to see than what's on the surface. Love causes us to look beyond what the physical eyes can see at first glance, and it opens us to a world beyond. Love unveils the presence of God and causes our eyes to shift their focus and look further in. But this kind of seeing is always a choice. Jacques Lusseyran had learned by the time he was eight years old that the light within him would dim dramatically if he became caught in judgment or bitterness. He had learned that the light became brighter when his heart was filled with love.

Just as a 14-year-old girl once stood transfixed before a shop window, we, too, are invited to look beyond the surface of, well, everything. Learning to see not just with our physical eyes but with hearts attuned to love, compassion, and the inner light of God, is a life-long adventure. Like the woman who anointed Jesus' feet while the others remained clueless, we often miss the sacred right in front of us. True sight requires more than visual clarity; it cultivates attentiveness, curiosity, and connection to divine love. Whether it's people, nature, or ordinary moments of washing the dishes, God's presence surrounds us. So let's pause, look again, and learn to see beyond the glass.

Practice

1. The power of "and." Practice looking at a person or something in nature, and pay attention to what you notice first. Such as, "They are smiling," or "This leaf is many shades of green."

2. As you continue to observe, allow your heart and your eyes to linger while asking the question, "and?" Look a little deeper. Name what you notice now. Maybe something like, "There's a sadness behind their eyes," or "The structure of the leaf reminds me of finger prints."

3. Continue to look more deeply while asking yourself, "and?" and see where your heart takes you. Imagine looking at a piece of paper and beginning by noticing that it's simply white, lined paper. As you ask "and," you could also say, "I see a tree. I see the people who made the paper in a factory, the lumberjack who cut down the tree. I see the sun shining on the tree causing it to grow and the rain that watered the roots. I see the birds nesting." As you allow your heart to see more deeply, you might notice that lingering changes what your physical eyes can see. You can continue this exercise throughout your day, training your eyes to look more deeply.

Reflection Questions

1. Time and patience is required to train yourself to see more deeply. How would this change your approach to life?

2. Are you someone who moves through life too quickly? What are you possibly missing by not slowing down?

3. When you observe other people, do you feel compassion or judgment? What is God's invitation?

Chapter 7
Waiting

It was my high school graduation, and I was feeling the exhilaration you'd expect from a liberated teenager who was being freed from the monotony of daily classes. The family came over to celebrate, and among the gifts was the quintessential rite-of-passage for every graduate: Dr. Seuss' timeless classic, *Oh, the Places You'll Go!* My cousin took the book, opened it with a wink, and began a theatrical reading that kept us all enthralled.

But as the story progressed, I found myself unexpectedly agitated when it reached the section entitled "The Waiting Place." This classic book describes this waiting place as the "most useless space," the place you want to avoid at all cost. The pictures on the page depict miserable, lost humans who are certainly not the ones we dream of becoming. The words go like this:

"The waiting place, where people are just waiting.
Waiting for a train to go or a bus to come,
or a plane to go or the mail to come,
or the rain to go or the phone to ring,
or the snow to snow or waiting around for a Yes or No
or waiting for their hair to grow.
Everyone is just waiting.
Waiting for the fish to bite
or waiting for wind to fly a kite
or waiting around for Friday night
or waiting, perhaps, for their Uncle Jake
or a pot to boil, or a Better Break
or a string of pearls, or a pair of pants
or a wig with curls, or Another Chance.
Everyone is just waiting."[24]

Dr. Seuss isn't the only one who has demonized waiting. Paulo Coelho said "Waiting is painful. Forgetting is painful. But not knowing which to do is the worst kind of suffering."[25] And Tom Petty blessed us with the lyric, "The waiting is the hardest part."[26] It seems, in fact, to be near the top of the pile of the most horrible things that could transpire in a single day. Our culture has despised the idea of waiting so much that we have nearly erased its necessity altogether. If we're honest, most of us are relieved that we now have hand-held computers that have made idle waiting a faint memory of the long-ago past. We may even brag about how much work we can get done on our phones while we are forced to wait for an oil change. Walk into any waiting

---

24   Dr. Seuss, *Oh, the Places You'll Go!* (Random House, 1990).
25   Paulo Coelho, *By the River Piedra I Sat Down and Wept* (HarperOne, 2021).
26   Tom Petty and the Heartbreakers, "The Waiting," *Hard Promises* album produced by Tom Petty and Jimmy Lovine, 1981.

room and just take a look around. Ninety-nine percent of the time, every person in the room will have their faces lost in their phones. When was the last time you actually had to wait when you allowed yourself to just sit *waiting* and not *do* anything to pass the time?

Time. Humans have a complex relationship with time. We organize our days around time, define ourselves by how we spend our time, set priorities and make plans based on the knowledge that time will pass, allocating our time accordingly. We develop strategies to make the most of our time, such as creating schedules, setting deadlines, and using productivity tools, usually trying to help us become more effective. Then we need other tools, teachings and books, to unlearn our obsession with constant stimulation, so we preach about returning to the practice of Sabbath and the value of rest to help us undo all this effort. But now we need to schedule the time to do all of this resting, and maybe take a class on how to actually rest, since we have clearly forgotten. Yes, waiting has become a lost art. It's just a faint memory in our frazzled, overloaded lives. Maybe Dr. Seuss had more influence than we gave him credit for.

The Bible is filled with exhortations such as, "Wait for the LORD; be strong, and let your heart take courage; wait for the LORD!" (Psalm 27:14 ESV). I recently overheard someone try to encourage a suffering soul with this verse, and I felt a snort slip out of my lips over the severity of our denial. Do we even know what it is to wait anymore? The action of waiting has been methodically and intentionally blotted from our lives, so what makes us think that we know what to do with this verse? It's no wonder that we have a desperate confusion about hearing the voice of God. We are told, "But they soon forgot his works; they did not wait for his counsel" (Psalm 106:13 ESV). I wonder how our determination to avoid all kinds of waiting has crippled our ability to listen, and therefore, our ability to hear. There are some things you just can't schedule. The exhortations to wait upon the Lord are replete throughout the Bible, and I'm not sure if we know what this means, let alone how to do it.

The story of Simeon in Luke chapter 2 gives us a glimpse of waiting. Simeon is known in Church tradition as the God-receiver. Isn't that beautiful? It's honestly the theme of this whole book. May we all learn how to be God-receivers. We don't know for certain if Simeon had any official role in the temple, but we do know that he lived for one thing—to see the Lord's Christ. The story goes that the Holy Spirit had told Simeon he would not die until he saw the Lord's Christ with his own eyes. On the day that Mary and Joseph brought Jesus to the temple to present Him to the Lord, Simeon was led by the Spirit to come to the temple. He took one look at this infant, took him in his arms, and said:

> *"Now Lord, You are releasing Your bond-servant to depart in peace, according to Your word; for my eyes have seen Your salvation, which You have prepared in the presence of all peoples, A LIGHT OF REVELATION TO THE GENTILES, and the glory of Your people Israel"* (Luke 2:29 32 NASB1995).

Some of the oldest Christian traditions hold that Simeon had already lived an unnaturally long life, over 200 years, by the time that Christ was born. He had been watching, listening, and waiting for a very long time. Other than the shepherds and Mary and Joseph, Simeon was the first to recognize the infant as the Messiah. But he had no angels, no stars to follow, and no careful decoding of the prophecy to guide him. It doesn't seem as though Joseph and Mary had a conversation with him when he entered. So why was the truth of Jesus so clear to him? The only thing that the Bible tells us is that he had spent a long time perfecting the art of waiting, and dare I say longing.

I believe Simeon is a prophetic picture for the Body of Christ. We are living in the in between, the now and the not-yet. We have believed in Jesus, following Him wholeheartedly, and now we are waiting for His return. Waiting is in the core DNA of what it means to be a believer in Jesus. Yet, our waiting muscles have atrophied.

If we want to hear God, to perceive His presence, and to know His leading, His love, and His ways, we must learn how to sit in a posture of quiet waiting in His presence. He will not allow us to relate to Him as a slot machine, expecting Him to speak on demand. Learning to open our hearts, lay down our agendas, and teach our souls to wait upon Him is foundational to our discipleship, and most certainly a vital aspect of all prayer. But our vocation as Jesus followers goes beyond this. We are to be a waiting people. Waiting isn't to be a temporary practice, but rather a constant posture of our hearts.

> *"But they who wait for the LORD shall renew their strength; they shall mount up with wings like eagles; they shall run and not be weary; they shall walk and not faint"* (Isaiah 40:31 ESV).

> *"When those that wait on the Lord mount up with wings like eagles, they were not literally waiting to mount up on eagles' wings. They were waiting on the Lord, and in the meantime, they flew like eagles. That makes me think that waiting for the Lord is when we are most alive. Maybe this is saying that when we're waiting is when we soar, because it is also when we long, when we are captivated, and when we are most in love."*[27]

---

27   Joe Spann, poet and elder at Believers Church, Tulsa OK.

Love waits with hope. Love listens patiently, even to the silence of the long waiting. We're not just waiting on a specific answer to prayer, but we are called to live our lives with expectant, waiting hearts. Not the kind of passive, distracted waiting we think of most of the time, but the expectant, vigilant, passionate kind of waiting. This kind of waiting is the soil of longing.

Many of us relate to the sense of longing as if it's a problem that needs to be fixed. Much like we relate to our own needs. When we have a need, most of us can find ways to meet it. If we can't satisfy the need, we become agitated.

But what if we could learn to relate to our needs and longings as some of the greatest gifts we've been given? What if the felt sense of our need is the proof of love, and therefore, the awareness of our need that produces an ache, a longing, actually becomes our meeting place with God? We have tried and have quite nearly convinced ourselves that we succeeded at satiating our every need, avoiding the feeling of longing all together. But what do we sacrifice when we deny the existence of our longing? The essence of being poor in spirit *is* being in need. The first sentence Jesus spoke within the most famous teaching of all time was, "Blessed are the poor in spirit, for theirs is the kingdom of heaven" (Matthew 5:3 ESV). Our need *is* the place we encounter the Kingdom of heaven, so why do we relate to all forms of need, lack, or longing as if they're the sign of a terrible problem?

As Johannes Baptist Metz says, "We are all beggars. We are all members of a species that is not sufficient unto itself. We are all creatures plagued by unending doubts and restless, unsatisfied hearts. Of all creatures, we are the poorest and the most incomplete. Our needs are always beyond our capacities, and we only find ourselves when we lose ourselves."[28]

---

28   Johannes Baptist Metz, *Poverty of Spirit* (Paulist Press, Kindle Edition, 1998) 25.

As I come to terms with and begin to embrace my inherent need, I allow my vulnerable soul to exist without criticism, transforming it into a gateway for experiencing His love. This shift in perspective liberates me to be authentically human in His presence, creating space for love to emerge from my need. This love materializes as a profound yearning, serving as a prophetic beacon illuminating the path ahead.

My friend, poet and elder at our church, Joe Spann, wrote one of my favorite writings of all time on waiting. I'd like to share a section of it:

"In our culture, it is entirely possible for all but the poorest and sickest of us to live a life in which every whim, every simple appetite is immediately satiated. Never an ache that goes unmedicated, never a moment where our mood cannot be suited by the music we want, the entertainment we want, the temperature we want. Our clothes, our occupation, our friends, even our faces can be changed at will. And so we have developed a very human but very insidious habit: we scratch every itch.

"We are the itch scratchers. Behold our cultural identity. Itch-scratchers devote themselves dutifully day after day: changing this, tweaking that, surfing from one appetite to the next. Itch-scratchers all look down. Down at our screens, down at our watches, down at the road, down at our clothes, our jobs, our itches. Now more than ever it is possible to keep our heads down and our days filled. And as long as we can keep the silence at bay and the emptiness far away, we can convince ourselves that we are making some sort of progress. And therein lies the plot of the enemy. He lulls us into the dream-sleep of too weak desires. And

as long as we are scratching today's itch, we are too busy for too long, and we can be satisfied by lesser gods.

"We need no healing as long as we stay comfortable. We need no savior as long as we have a cozy drink by the fireplace. We need no birthright when a bowl of soup or a latte will suffice for now.

"The itch-scratcher is never empty. He is never waiting or longing like Simeon. He is always full, never mourns, never hungers or thirsts. The itch-scratcher knows the touch of so many lovers that purity no longer seems desirable.

"But the itch-scratcher cannot wait and never experiences the longing we are made for. Longing is the invasion point of God's Kingdom in our world. Longing is the beachhead at Normandy. Longing is where eternity touches time.

"When I say longing, I need to clarify something. I am not talking about a craving or an appetite or a mood. I am talking about something that may be somewhat unfamiliar to us itch-scratchers. You won't find it on the GPS; there is no 'app for that.' Longing is a sacred ground on the far side of poverty, the far side of hunger, the far side of grief. The journey there will cost you something. It is a desperation you feel in your bones at the edge of a hole that is too deep to ever be filled; a ground so close to the edge of madness that going there may leave you unfit for normal daily life."

The word *wait* in Hebrew is *qavah*, (kaw-vaw).[29] It has both a literal (straight forward) and a figurative (implied or symbolic) meaning. The literal meaning of *qavah* is "to bind or twist together strands of a rope (entwine, probably originally twist, stretch, then of tension of enduring, waiting)." The figurative meaning of *qavah* is "expecting, hoping, waiting, anticipating."

As we wait, anticipate, and trust in God, we are not to passively twiddle our thumbs. We are to engage in a deep process of binding, twisting, and entwining our lives with the Father, Son, and Holy Spirit. We hold our hearts in waiting with an open heart and mind, patiently observing, seeking, and listening *with* God, giving Him our full attention.

Attention is truly the rarest form of generosity, don't you think? We give Him our attention in our times of silence and solitude, or during our morning prayers, but giving Him our attention can become a way of life. This kind of waiting is all about the long game—it's a lifelong pilgrimage. We are always learning, practicing, and becoming in this relationship with God, and waiting will weave itself into our DNA in the process, if we allow it.

I don't think Simeon was perfect in his waiting, so I'm sure we won't be either. We can assume he had impatient, irritable days as well as battles with unbelief, simply because he was human. But the practice itself will change us, there's no doubt about that. May the Lord forever teach us how to hold our hearts entwined with Him, waiting, longing, and anticipating as we go throughout our days. And if you struggle with understanding and dealing with unanswered prayer, *God on Mute* by Pete Greig is one of the best books I've read on this topic. Please consider adding it to your library to help you make sense of this aspect of prayer.

29   "6960. Qavah," *BibleHub.com*, 2025, https://biblehub.com/hebrew/6960.htm.

Hearing God will always require waiting. We can't demand that He speaks to us when we're finally sitting with our coffee and Bible. It is not honoring to God to give Him a window of time to speak to us—in the morning or an hour on Sunday—because we are finally present. Our aim must be greater than that. We engage with God on His terms, and that means cultivating a life of listening, waiting, and longing for the One we love.

"I remain confident of this: I will see the goodness of the LORD in the land of the living. Wait for the LORD; be strong and take heart and wait for the LORD" (Psalm 27:13-14 NIV).

Practice

Settle into silence for one or two minutes.

- Find a quiet place.

- Sit comfortably, close your eyes, and take a few deep breaths.

- Release distractions with each exhale.

Pick a word or phrase that expresses your desire to wait on God, such as:

Wait

Here I am

Be still

I trust You

These word(s) will be your gentle anchor when your thoughts drift.

Enter into a period of silence, maybe 8 to 10 minutes. Silently introduce your sacred word as a symbol of your openness to God. Whenever you notice your thoughts pulling you away, gently return to your word/phrase. Rest in the presence of God with no agenda or striving. Just be.

"I wait for the Lord, my soul waits, and in His word I hope."
Psalm 130:5 ESV

Gently return your attention to your breath. Offer a short prayer like: Lord, I trust in Your timing. Help me to wait with hope.

Open your eyes and sit in stillness a moment before moving on.

Reflection Questions

1. Can you recall a season in your life when you had to wait on God? What was that experience like for you emotionally and spiritually?

2. How do you typically respond to waiting—with frustration, peace, anxiety, or trust? Why do you think that is?

3. What might God be forming in you during a time of waiting?

4. Have you seen fruit or transformation in your life that came specifically from a time of prolonged waiting?

Chapter 8
Darkness

"To know the dark, go dark. Go without sight, and find that the dark, too, blooms and sings."
—Wendell Berry

Determined to live our lives beyond the small town boundaries of Findlay, Ohio, Craig and I ventured forth to the shores of Southern California soon after he put a ring on my finger. Many evenings after watching the sunset, we would find ourselves laying on the beach admiring the gradual emergence of the stars. There was something so magical about listening to the dark ocean waves crashing not far from our feet while watching the stars come out of hiding one by one.

The ocean held a different power at night. Maybe because I couldn't see as far, the ferocity of the waves felt more intimidating. I remember shuddering with a twinge of fear every now and then as

I felt its intensity, and I wondered why the waves felt more ominous in the dark. I would talk myself through the reality that it was only because my vision was limited. I was listening to the same beautiful waves I had watched earlier that day. It was the same water, and the same familiar sand was under my feet, yet I had to push back fear more than once so that I could enjoy the majesty spread out before me.

I think back on this now, and I realize how often I still feel fear simply because I can't see. Why does vision help me feel safe? Why does knowledge of what is in front of me feel as if I have some kind of control over it?

Darkness is a word in our culture that has evolved with nearly universal symbolism—basically, it is synonymous with bad. Just say the word and the associations begin to flow: death, devil, evil, criminal, danger, doubt, depression, loss, fear. A lot of fear. Early in my Christian faith journey, I would hear people discuss the dark night of the soul in hushed tones and knowing glances. It felt like code for the worst thing you could say about anyone. All I knew was that it sent shivers down my spine. So, I bought the famous book by John of the Cross and read it cover to cover. I wouldn't recommend this book for a brand new, fresh out of the baptismal waters believer, but it certainly left its mark. I'm not sure how much of the book I actually understood, because I was just looking for the terrible bits. Those were the parts of the Christian journey I wanted to avoid. That reading strategy is not an approach to reading John of the Cross that I would recommend. The book ended up in the hazardous pile with the rest of the things that people used the word "dark" to describe.

If I could change anything about the early foundations of my faith, this would be on the top of the list. It wasn't helpful to have such an ingrained framework for darkness built within my psyche at the very start. It has taken nearly 30 years to unlearn this mindset and bring redemption to the dark.

In the beginning, God created the heavens and separated the day from the night, giving honor to both. We desperately need the night, and I feel eternally grateful for its literal, time-boundaried relief of the hot sun, as well as the metaphorical aspects of the word *dark*. I have learned things in the dark that I could never have learned in the light—things that have changed me forever, in the best kind of way.

> *I will give you the treasures of darkness and the riches hidden in secret places, so that you may know that I am the LORD, the God of Israel, who calls you by name.* (Isaiah 45:3 BSB)

Anyone who has journeyed with the Lord for any length of time will echo their appreciation for the treasures they've received in the dark. You can hear it in the voices of those who have suffered greatly and can say with holy humility that they were thankful for the appearance of darkness in their lives, even though they wouldn't wish it upon anyone. God does holy work in the darkness. There are treasures to be found when our addiction to light is confronted.

It's helpful to take a journey through Scripture to see all the beauty and power that happened in the dark. Jacob saw a ladder with angels ascending and descending in the dark of the night. Elijah's encounter with God's still small voice was at night. The Israelites were delivered from slavery in the dark of the night. And let's remember, Jesus' birth was announced to the shepherds at night.

But there's more. We see the wise men guided by a star directing them to a newborn Jesus, Paul and Silas were delivered from prison, shepherds were visited by angels, Peter was visited by an angel in prison, and Paul's blindness was healed. The transfiguration of Jesus may have occurred in the dark since the disciples were struggling to stay awake, the Last Supper was shared, and probably the most significant event that happened in utter darkness was the resurrection of Jesus, which happened in a damp, gloomy cave, alone in the dark.

Life grows in dark places. The life of a seed begins buried deep in the soil, the life of a baby is tucked inside a mother's womb, and many species of mushrooms and plants need dark, damp caves for survival. Many deep-sea creatures, such as anglerfish, giant tube worms, and giant squid thrive in the dark depths of the ocean where sunlight doesn't reach. Maybe darkness isn't all that bad, after-all.

As I've shared in a previous chapter, I've had my own seasons where all seemed to go dim, where the voice of God not only seemed quiet, but absent altogether. Diving into readings about the dark night of the soul later in my pilgrimage was very helpful. Gerald May's book has been my favorite so far. He helped me reframe not only how I saw darkness, but how I related to it emotionally.

He said, "The dark night is a profoundly good thing. It is an ongoing spiritual process in which we are liberated from attachments and compulsions and empowered to live and love more freely. Sometimes this letting go of old ways is painful, occasionally even devastating. But this is not why the night is called 'dark.' The darkness of the night implies nothing sinister, only that the liberation takes place in hidden ways, beneath our knowledge and understanding. It happens mysteriously, in secret, and beyond our conscious control. For that reason it can be disturbing or even scary, but in the end it always works to our benefit."[30]

Sometimes God leads us into the darkness of the cave, which is often experienced through sensory deprivation, in order to expose our

---

30   Gerald May, MD, *The Dark Night of the Soul* (HarperCollins Kindle Edition, 2009), 4-5.

attachments and set us free. It is nearly impossible for humans not to build fortified castle walls around the things we think we know. When God speaks to us a certain way enough times, we begin to feel as though we have it nailed down. We may even teach classes on listening for God in this particular way, encouraging others to learn from the expertise we have learned.

But He will not allow our juvenile over-confidence to remain intact. We naturally become overly dependent upon a *way* of meeting with Him, which is far too narrow for the expansiveness of God. Our well-worn ruts of favorite prayer rhythms, approaches, spiritual disciplines, and methods will inevitably cease working, and I'm so glad they do. They don't fail us just because we become bored, but because we become overly confident and captivated by the method itself.

Intimacy in a relationship can never be tied down to a method, or it will suffocate. Spiritual disciplines are helpful and necessary, yet when they become containers for God with expectations attached, we need to be set free from the methods themselves. God, in His mercy and kindness, will stop gracing these ruts with His tangible presence, which creates an uncomfortable, internal crisis. The crisis looks different within us all, with our varied personalities. Some will feel abandoned by God and need to dive into the brokenness behind this perspective. Others will feel frustrated that God isn't holding up His end of the bargain and will need to work through the reality of their powerlessness.

No matter what your emotional response is to the shift of God's presence and grace, just know that the storm stirred up within you is the point. These moments of crisis are divine invitations to journey into the dark of the cave where internal transformation crashes its way into dusty corners you didn't know existed.

"At first, people usually try to recreate their old ways of prayer and living. Over time and with repeated failures, however, they recognize that such attempts come from a sense of obligation or sheer habit, not from real desire. Though they are loath to admit it, they gradually realize that they lack the motivation they once had for focused meditation and effortful striving in their lives, work, and relationships. In honesty, they come to acknowledge they really don't want to return to the old ways. This can be more troubling than the lack of accomplishment, because it feels like a lack of caring. 'The soul,' John (of the cross) says, 'turns to God with painful concern, thinking it is not serving God but turning away.' It feels like a betrayal of God, of one's friends and enterprises, and of one's own soul. The painfulness of this realization, according to John, is an important sign that the dryness is not due to laxity or lukewarmness, in which there is no such concern. The person has by no means forgotten God, but rather remembers God with great pain and grief."[31]

Throughout these transformative periods, God works within us in numerous ways, one of which is often for the training of our heart to trust Him in the silence. We become painfully aware that we are not in control of when He speaks, how He speaks, or if He will speak at all. We are receivers. When we finally cease striving, He will lead us to stillness and peace in the dark. In stillness, we wait for our soul to settle in the knowing of His love, regardless of what He allows us to feel or not feel, hear or not hear, see or not see.

I do *not* believe God plays hide and seek with us. I don't know where this terrible teaching had its beginnings, but I'd like to squash it once and for all.

---

31   Gerald May, MD, *The Dark Night of the Soul* (HarperCollins Kindle Edition, 2009), 140.

"I love those who love me, and those who seek me find me"
(Proverbs 8:17 NIV).
"'I will be found by you,'" declares the LORD"
(Jeremiah 29:14 NIV).

"Ask and it will be given to you; seek and you will find; knock and the door will be opened to you" (Matthew 7:7 NIV).

"Never will I leave you; never will I forsake you"
(Hebrews 13:5 NIV).

The incarnation alone is proof that God is not about the business of playing hide and seek. What does happen, though, is that we grow accustomed to looking for Him in certain ways, expecting Him to meet us in the same ways He has before, and our vision narrows. This must be confronted within us in order for our awareness of God to deepen and our ideas of God to expand.

Other attachments that are confronted in the darkness are false identities, masks, walls of self protection, pretenses, personal image and reputation, hyper spirituality, the confines of religion, etc. The list is nearly endless. Our truest identities are carved out in the dark. Our God is a Master Sculptor, carefully carving us out of a large clump of clay, casting off the extra bits that are cloaking our genuine selves. We may kick and scream, but in the end, we will learn to trust the hand of the Artist and surrender to the work of the dark.

By this time, you may be thinking of the Bible verses that refer to God as light (see 1 John 1:5). This is true, of course. But what is *also* true is that, "The LORD has said that he would dwell in thick darkness" (1 Kings 8:12 ESV). When the Israelites sent Moses up the mountain to talk with God, they watched him enter the darkness (see

Exodus 20:21). Psalm 97:2 tells us that "clouds and thick darkness are all around him."

There are many different kinds of darkness. Some, indeed, are the evil kind. The kind of oppression that is brought on by sinister spiritual forces. Some forms of darkness come from within our own soul as we work through our personal hang ups and issues. Some darknesses are the intentional isolation of a prayer cave, while other kinds are the terrifying hand of suffering. Then, of course, sometimes darkness comes from the holiness of the dark night of the soul. But God is *within* them all. As the psalmist states clearly and poetically,

> *Where can I go from Your Spirit?*
> *Or where can I flee from Your presence?*
> *If I ascend to heaven, You are there;*
> *If I make my bed in Sheol, behold, You are there.*
> *If I take the wings of the dawn,*
> *If I dwell in the remotest part of the sea,*
> *Even there Your hand will lead me,*
> *And Your right hand will lay hold of me.*
> *If I say, "Surely the darkness will overwhelm me,*
> *And the light around me will be night,"*
> *Even the darkness is not dark to You,*
> *And the night is as bright as the day.*
> *Darkness and light are alike to You.*
> (Psalm 139:7-12 NASB)

> *"For I am sure that neither death nor life, nor angels nor*
> *rulers, nor things present nor things to come, nor powers, nor*
> *height nor depth, nor anything else in all creation, will be able*

to separate us from the love of God in Christ Jesus our Lord"
(Romans 8:38-39 ESV).

Whatever the source of the darkness you encounter, it's important that you remember that no darkness is dark to the Lord. He still sees even when you can't. The crashing waves of the sea at night are the same waves you loved in the light of day, but now you are invited to trust Him in the dimness of your senses. The journey is to *know* Him, not just to *hear* Him. The purpose is to become increasingly aware of Him in the midst of the cloud of unknowing—to learn how to fling your heart open wide, especially when you cannot see and cannot hear. This is what it means to keep your lamp burning through the night (see Matthew 25:1–13).

I will leave you with this prayer from Thomas Merton.

"My Lord God, I have no idea where I am going. I do not see the road ahead of me. I cannot know for certain where it will end. Nor do I really know myself, and the fact that I think I am following your will does not mean that I am actually doing so. But I believe that the desire to please you does in fact please you. And I hope I have that desire in all that I am doing. I hope that I will never do anything apart from that desire. And I know that if I do this you will lead me by the right road, though I may know nothing about it. Therefore I will trust you always though I may seem to be lost and in the shadow of death. I will not fear, for you are ever with me, and you will never leave me to face my perils alone."[32]

---

32   Thomas Merton, *Thoughts in Solitude* (Farrar, Straus and Giroux, 1999).

Practice

1. Try to create for yourself a few moments of sensory deprivation. Choose a quiet room, close the blinds, and remove any electronics. In this place of solitude and no distractions, imagine yourself in His cave simply listening to His voice. Allow Him the freedom to show up as He desires. Think about:

    What are the ways that you typically expect Him to typically be with you?

    Ask Him to surprise you with His presence in ways not expected.

2. Imagine playing hide-and-seek with God. In this scenario, God is a great hider.

    Now, imagine Him stepping out from His hiding place to reveal Himself and embrace you. Stay in the moment to feel His pleasure as He relieves you of the pain of not seeing Him—of not feeling cherished during His absence.

3.   Write out a list of your known false identities, masks, self-pro-
      tection practices, and religious confines. Now ask God if there
      are other unknown limitations that you have that He would
      like to reveal to you.

Reflection Questions

1.   Do you feel abandoned by God? Why? When did you first
      realize it?

2.   Do you feel a storm brewing inside of you? See if you can
      identify the storm's origin.

3.   Are you remembering God with "great pain and grief"?

Chapter 9

Discernment

We use the word *discernment* in wide and various contexts these days, each of them carrying any number of meanings. The word has become a bit of a catchphrase. Most of our common uses of the word seem to be trying to describe a process of making decisions, choosing the best path, etc. But we say *discerning* instead of *thinking* because we're trying to make these decisions from a deeper place other than our rational minds. It's as if we are trying to give more meaning to the word *decide*—and we're right to do so. The word discern often means that we're trying to sense our way through something, not just *think* our way through something. As Christians, we usually use the word when we want to separate good from evil, right from wrong, or be aware of more sinister dynamics at play. But we should never just stop at trying to discern evil. At the end of the day, our goal should always be to discern what God is doing, speaking, or desiring.

As Jesus followers, we desire to follow God's leading in our daily lives. This means that we naturally want to grow in learning His ways, because at the core of being disciples is a calling to be a discerning people—a people who are following the voice of their Good Shepherd. This is also true when discussing the gift of discerning of spirits, which we will talk about in more detail later in this chapter. In both cases, we want to see true discernment stand in its rightful place in the Body of Christ. In order for this to happen, we need to understand the biblical purpose of discernment and cultivate a fresh imagination for how it functions in health and maturity.

Many people use the word discernment interchangeably with hearing the voice of God, primarily because of the sensory experience of both. I think the difference between the discernment and hearing/perceiving the voice of God is the purpose. The word discernment actually means "to separate."[33] It has the connotation of trying to separate and categorize pieces of information. If discernment was to stop at just trying to separate evil from good, you would be leaving out the need for God's wisdom in our response to the discernment.

The end goal of discernment must be to discern God, to sense His desire, His voice, and His direction, and this is why it leaks right into the broader conversation of hearing His voice. As we have discussed in previous chapters, the practice of discernment, and/or perceiving, hearing, communing with the voice of God is experienced through all of our senses. This means that it will take time and effort to untangle all that may be happening simultaneously. It's not simple or easy to distinguish between our thoughts, emotions, reactions, conclusions, or what may be true spiritual discernment. Then, when we recognize that along with a spiritual element, there is also a natural element to discernment, it gets even more challenging to steward. Amidst what

---

33   "1252. Diakronó," *BibleHub.com*, 2025, https://biblehub.com/greek/1252.htm.

is often a swirl of sensory input and human responses to that input, God also reveals His wisdom. Learning to discern His voice, warning, direction, or instruction through the many things you sense and feel is challenging.

As I pondered the best analogy to use in unpacking the experience of discernment, I thought about lasagna. I may be hankering for Italian food, but I think it'll work. Lasagna is a tasty pasta dish that has many layers. When served on your plate, you can see some of the layers, and some of the layers are less noticeable. Yet your senses will take in the experience of all the ingredients as they blend together. In a similar way, most people who experience spiritual discernment are often only aware of the whole mix of presenting sensations blended together.

Our growth journey into mature discernment is like learning how to take a finished lasagna and peel back the layers bit by bit, observing all the things involved in the sensory experience. It's necessary to take note of all the different ingredients, noticing what was mixed and baked into its current state. As we peel apart the layers, naming each piece as best we can, we will focus on both the external bits of information we're taking in, as well as the internal dynamics of processing all the bits of information.

It's usually not wise to try to overly define the mysterious, illusive, intangible things of the unseen world. So please grant me some wiggle room as I try to bring a little clarity to a couple of different elements of the experience of discernment. For the sake of this conversation, I'm going to refer to the "natural" and the "supernatural." Even as I write these words, I am struggling with their lack of separateness. The supernatural overlaps and infills what we would think of as the natural world. So, I'm very resistant to drawing hard lines between things that are beautifully, rightfully entangled. Yet, it does feel important to put words to varying realities, especially as we try to understand the experience, function, and purpose of discernment.

For the sake of this discussion, when I say "natural," I am referring to the human, physical, and even scientific dimension of discernment, both tangible and intangible. When I say "supernatural," I am referring to the spiritual world that we see in Scripture, such as the angelic, demonic, the activity of the Holy Spirit, and interaction with God, Himself. Regarding discernment, I believe we experience both the natural and the supernatural.

Natural

Most of us can relate to experiencing a change in atmosphere when someone who is angry walks into the room. Or we may refer to someone "lighting up the room" because his or her joy seems to reach out and touch nearly everyone present. In the conversation of discernment, I believe it's helpful to discuss these experiences in deeper ways. We all understand these things at some level because they are common experiences. But we rarely discuss the why or how of these moments. Maybe it's because we are uncomfortable discussing mysterious things we can't wrap our minds around more rationally. Yet many of these experiences are very human, physical realities.

Most people can sense, to some degree, what other people are feeling. Some are more naturally sensitive than others. But when we stop to think about it, we are usually more aware of the emotions of others than we acknowledge. For instance, many of us have had the experience of knowing that someone was angry or sad when he or she walked into the room. So when we discuss feeling other people's emotions, we are having a very human, physical experience. To call this discernment isn't inaccurate, but it may be incomplete.

The sensations someone feels from others are only one very small element in the discussion of discernment. What are we truly feeling, and what do these sensory experiences actually tell us? We may discern, sense, or feel that someone is angry as he enters a room, but that doesn't tell us very much. We do not know why he is angry. In reality, we do not know for a fact that he is angry. Anger, pain, or irritation could manifest in similar ways. Do we really know what this person is feeling? All we know for certain is that we're feeling something emanating from them that could be anger. It's actually not a provable fact without a conversation with the person in which he confirms his anger.

We must remind ourselves that only God knows the heart of a person. Holding these sensory moments gently and maintaining a respectful awareness of what remains unknown is crucial in mature discernment. Human emotions are very complex. Presuming we know more than we do based on something we're sensing physically is always a mistake. When we presume to know the motives of another, we have stepped into the essence of unhealthy judgment. Yet, I believe we can glean much wisdom, compassion, and relational maturity from learning to increase our awareness of the emotional state of others for the sake of compassion and kindness.

Another example of "natural" discernment could be the ability to notice micro-expressions. These could be facial twitches, slight body language changes, etc. There is an imperfect science that can be helpful in noticing when someone is lying, for instance. Some people are naturally or instinctively perceptive in this area. In fact, most of us have some of these abilities and may not know that we rely upon visible expressions for clues.

Certain personalities are more sensitive and naturally discerning in these ways. Some personalities are instinctually heart, or emotion-centered, while others are more thought, or intellect-centered. The emotion-centered personalities will be more accustomed to sensing other people's emotions, but may have a challenging time separating their own emotions in the mix. The intellect-centered personalities may be more intuitive to micro-expressions, body language, and other sensory input. This doesn't mean that intellect-centered people don't experience the impact of other's emotional presence, or visa-versa. It just means that your personality will influence your natural strengths and weaknesses.

Many people who have heightened sensory sensitivity have learned this ability from early childhood as a means of assessing the safety of their surroundings. Children in homes where there is violence or addiction have often strengthened their senses as a means of self-protection. If their safety hinged upon another person's emotions, for instance, they would instinctively learn what anger felt like when it entered a room. But this doesn't mean that they are automatically sensitive to all emotions. Just because they have honed their ability to sense danger doesn't mean that they could just as easily sense desire or longing. In fact, they may have an overdeveloped, heightened antenna for danger, sometimes misleading them to search for it even when it doesn't exist. Simultaneously, they could have an underdeveloped sense of beauty and safety.

Another area of natural discernment is our vision/seeing. This seems obvious, but the more we lean into the topic of what we're seeing and how our brain is processing the data our eyes are receiving, it becomes less and less obvious. There are all kinds of studies about how convinced we can be that we saw something that didn't actually happen. It's also true that sometimes we see things that others don't see. Our eyes are prone to jump to quick conclusions, filling in gaps with our own assumptions. For example, how many of us as Jesus' followers could be in a brothel or a crack house and still sense the presence of God? Yet, learning how to see as God sees is the call of every believer. When matured, a true function of discernment, both naturally and supernaturally, will be viewing our surroundings through the eyes of our Creator.

Everyone can learn and grow in these areas of natural discernment. We can work to strengthen our awareness muscle with some intentional, deeper focus on others. In fact, I highly encourage you to do just that. Humans communicate with their whole being, and learning to perceive the unspoken dimensions of communication and rightly responding to what we're sensing will help strengthen our relationship skills significantly.

Supernatural

The spiritual gift of "Discerning of Spirits" is supernatural in nature. This means that its purpose and function are to be initiated, empowered, and guided by the Holy Spirit.

In the Bible, we read of Jesus (quoting Isaiah) saying, "The Spirit of the Lord is on me" (Luke 4:18). We also see Gideon experiencing the Spirit of God as if he was putting on a piece of clothing (see Judges 6:34), and the Spirit coming mightily upon David after the anointing of Samuel (see 1 Samuel 16:13). Experiences like these are scattered through the pages of the Bible. We also read of demonic spirits terrorizing Saul (see 1 Samuel 16:14-15), of the demoniac in the synagogue at Capernaum (see Mark 1:21-26), and of the Gadarene demoniac (see Matthew 8:28). To see these stories in Scripture and to conclude that these are experiential encounters seems evident. So, to consider the notion that people may sense angelic or demonic activity does not seem far-fetched.

I know many people with this gift, and they often find themselves overwhelmed with all they sense and feel as they walk into various places. What is happening in these moments is likely multifaceted. Both natural and supernatural atmospheres can feel tangible, but not always. Most often, from my own experience, this kind of sensory overload means that many things are happening simultaneously.

The Learning Curve

It was a beautiful sunny day as I pulled into the parking garage of the hospital. I was there to visit a friend who was having a small procedure done. I walked from the four-story parking garage into a glass walk-way that would take me to the hospital building. I was about halfway through the passage when I felt as if I had walked into a thick cloud of despair, and it stopped me in my tracks. I closed my eyes and waited. I could hear what seemed like faint, faraway voices of people crying out to God to heal their loved ones. I felt this on every level. All of my senses were jumping, and my emotions were responding. I walked to the window and looked down beneath the walkway, where I saw a small hospital chapel. I was instantly convinced that someone was in the chapel, and I was to go pray with them. So I ran back through the parking garage, found my way down the stairs, and approached the chapel. I opened the door, and there was no one there. I felt a wave of confusion as my mind retraced the experience, wondering if I had made the whole thing up. I checked in with the Lord and heard nothing. It's official, I thought. I'm going crazy. I shook my head in an attempt to reboot my rational brain and walked slowly back toward the hospital. I said a few obligatory prayers as I walked to my friend's room. Of course, I didn't tell her what had just happened.

The reality is that God hadn't actually told me anything. I felt some things, heard some things, and then made many assumptions. So what did I feel? What was I hearing? What was from God, and what was just the atmosphere? Was there something God was trying to show me, or was this just something in the air that my antenna picked up? This experience (and many others like it) caused me to step back from my automatic assumption and, instead, ask many more questions. I became like a four-year-old little girl who was constantly tugging on God's pant leg asking a gazillion questions about everything.

Herein lies the learning curve. If you can begin to separate and categorize some of what you're sensing, it may be helpful. Is it just an atmosphere? Is it someone's emotions or intentions emanating from them? Or is it spiritual in nature? What is going on within my own emotions as a response, and what is outside of me? Learning to separate these sensory moments is a part of exercising your discernment—but it is not the end goal. So far, this is just the data you are categorizing. It doesn't actually help you know what you are to *do* with this data. It's just information, and that is helpful to remember.

If we feel we are responsible for acting on every piece of information that our senses receive, we will become completely overwhelmed. Remind yourself that it's simply information, and not all information is worthy of your time and attention. Imagine walking into a New Year's Eve party right before midnight. The energy and anticipation in the room would be palpable and may even have a spiritual element in the mix. But you would have no need to react or respond to what you're sensing. What does matter, though, is your ability to be present in love, no matter what you're discerning. Your discernment is never allowed to hinder your love. You are an image-bearer of Christ Jesus, first and foremost.

What makes a space holy? What makes a space evil? I've felt the presence of God in a brothel, and I've been in church buildings that felt oppressive. Training our senses means that we aim to find Him everywhere we go. What is He doing? What is He dreaming? What is He longing for? The training of our soul is held in the trenches of finding eyes to see and ears to hear what the Holy Spirit is doing.

The Pause

Such a powerful tool. The power of pausing to take a breath before you react is profound. Pause when you feel overwhelmed with sensory input before you conclude anything. When you sense someone's emotions or spiritual darkness, pause before you react. This simple moment of pausing will give you time to detach yourself from the information you're receiving and check in with the Lord. Ask God: *Is this something You want me to pay attention to? Are You purposefully revealing something, or am I just an antenna picking things up? Am I supposed to do anything about this?* And remember, most things are more complicated than what you are sensing or perceiving in the moment.

There is a difference between picking things up with your spiritual antenna and hearing God's voice. There is a difference between feeling something in the atmosphere and receiving a direct revelation from God. It is a mistake to presume that everything we experience through our senses is an intentional revelation from God. This is freeing for many people to hear! It means that you are not responsible for responding to everything you are sensing. It means that you can learn to pull your antenna down and give your senses a break.

What matters is the will of God. This is what you want to discern. Sometimes getting an accurate read on the situation requires us to intentionally press through the noise of all the sensory input to discern what God is communicating, if anything at all. What is He saying? What is He doing? What does He want? Sensing things around you is not the point of discernment. Training our senses to discern *Him* is the point. As you mature in discernment, you will learn to know the difference between things you are just "picking up" and the intentional leading of the Spirit of God.

Whether you pause before or after observing your situation and your surroundings isn't the main consideration. What's most import-ant is that you intentionally take time to check in with your soul. You are most definitely in the mix, and that's okay. You cannot expect to be one hundred percent in the spirit or to remove your humanity out of the picture. You will sense and discern emotional and spiritual dynam-ics, and then your emotions will react to what you are discerning. It's unavoidable. Your thoughts, opinions, passions, values, and triggers will be in the mix.

These reactions are a part of our human experience. They aren't to be despised or demonized. But, we do need to grow in awareness of what is happening in our mind and emotions. Growth in discern-ment is directly linked to our journey with self-awareness. Learning to discern and steward our soul is a significant part of our growth into maturity. It's also necessary for our character development. We are human beings: spirit, soul, and body. Our whole being matters and is called to take part in our discernment.

Yet, your humanity is both a gift and a complexity. Being honest and aware of what is happening within you is where most of the learning curve transpires. It is crucial that you know yourself well enough to see that you really did sense/feel/perceive something and then your emotions reacted a certain way due to past pain, fear, etc. It doesn't demean you or diminish the importance of what you are perceiving, but it will go a long way in helping you properly discern the will of God.

Often, the first thing our senses perceive is negative. Negative emotions, issues, or oppressions are the easiest to pick up through our senses. If there's anger or lust in the room, discerners will feel it. If there is pornography or bitterness around, most sensitive types will perceive it. In the early days of experiencing these unpleasant sensory moments, reacting and jumping to quick conclusions will be easy.

In the early 2000s, we had a large house church that met in our home every Saturday night. We had an open-door policy for anyone who wanted to come and experience a meal, community, prayer, and worship. We regularly had somewhere between 50 to 80 people crammed into our home, with at least half of those between ages 2 and 17. On one of these nights, the house was particularly full. People were milling about with food in their hands, and all the conversations made for a loud and lively home. I was standing in the kitchen surrounded by people when I saw a stranger walk in the front door, amble down the hallway, and step into the living room. As he walked by, I felt an overwhelming wave of sexual perversion. I concluded several things immediately (nearly subconsciously) and avoided him the whole evening.

As the worship time came to a close, my husband asked if anyone wanted prayer. This guy raised his hand and said, "Yes, please. I spent the whole day today counseling and praying for a man caught in some pretty dark sexual perversion. It felt demonic and very heavy. I don't understand it, but I feel a bit slimed and deeply troubled by all I heard. I came here tonight because a friend told me you would know how to pray for me." Conviction hit me in the gut like a bowling ball. My senses perceived something that felt slimy, I drew instant conclusions, and proceeded to harshly judge this stranger. The Holy Spirit convicted me so strongly that I could hardly move as He showed me (yet again) just how complex these moments can be.

We know *in part*. We always know just a part of the picture. This should cultivate a deep humility within us all—but we often forget. It's easy to fall into the trap of presumption when our feelings are so strong. Gathering information about other people is not the point. If we are only grabbing hold of data for our own good, we clearly need more understanding about this gift.

> *"Do nothing out of selfish ambition or vain conceit. Rather, in humility value others above yourselves, not looking to your own interests but each of you to the interests of the others"* (Philippians 2:3-4 NIV).

Presuming we know more than we do without taking the time to sort through our heart reactions will leave us lacking in wisdom and often falling into judgment. Our growth will be found when we learn to cultivate dependence upon His voice, guidance, and wisdom, continually growing in the knowledge of His love and His ways.

The purpose and aim of all discernment is to discern the will of God. As we do the work of peeling back the layers, we aim to get to a place where we can hear, sense, see, and follow Him. True discernment takes time. Learn to honor the process as an intimate and holy space with God. God transforms us as He moves through us to accomplish His purposes. He is our center. He is ever-present, is always involved, and His will is perfect. All outcomes are in His hands.

As the famous monk Macarius said, "Secure the anchor rope to the rock and by the grace of God the ship will ride the devilish waves of the beguiling sea." He then explained his meaning: "The ship is your heart; keep guard over it. The rope is your mind; secure it to our Lord Jesus Christ, who is the rock who has power over all the waves."[34] Our humble response to an ever-increasing self-awareness and God-awareness is a growing dependence upon the Lord.

---

34   "There's No Such Thing as Ordinary," *GlobalAwakening.com*, 2025, https://globalawak-ening.com/there-s-no-such-thing-as-ordinary/.

"And this I pray, that your love may abound still more and more in real knowledge and all discernment" (Philippians 1:9 NASB).

I love that as Paul prays this prayer, he says "in." I like to think of it in this way: Within my knowledge, may love abound. Within my discernment, may love abound. So if I get a revelation of any kind, the call of the Lord is for love to abound inside of that revelation. Which, of course, makes sense, because God is love.

Practice

Sit quietly, close your eyes and take deep, long breaths. Ask the Lord to help you discern your heart clearly and courageously. Open your heart wide, allowing yourself to be seen and known by God, laying down all self protection and performance. If you sense a temptation to close your heart and pull away, resist by saying the following verses as a prayer slowly and repetitively, reminding yourself who God is:

> *"Love is patient and kind; love does not envy or boast;*
> *It is not arrogant or rude. It does not insist on its own way;*
> *it is not irritable or resentful; it does not rejoice at wrongdoing,*
> *but rejoices with the truth. Love bears all things,*
> *believes all things, hopes all things,*
> *endures all things. Love never ends"*
> (1 Corinthians:13:4–8 ESV).

Reflection Questions

1. Do you remember a time when you knew you were discerning something but you could tell that other things were in the mix? Maybe you also felt triggered or fearful of something at the same time.

2. Is there something you are discerning right now that you could spend some time with, naming various layers of internal and external realities at play?

3. How powerful do you feel in the midst of discerning through complex situations?

4. Do you feel victimized by your perceptions, or are you able to lean in more deeply to discern God's presence?

Chapter 10
Faith and Doubt

"Doubt doesn't alienate you from the divine,
it often means you're approaching it."[35]

I'm a doubter of God's voice. I'm also a believer that I hear His voice. Most often both of these are happening within me at the same time. There have been times I have been very confident that I heard God's voice only to find out that I was terribly wrong. Then I wondered if I had ever heard His voice at all and if I had imagined everything. I have spent my entire adult life talking about the voice of God and teaching others to hear Him, sense Him, and see Him. I have often found myself sharing with others what I felt He was saying. And most days I'm still very uncertain about everything I've ever said. Worse yet, I don't know if this is terrible insecurity or true, humble wisdom.

---

35   Cole Arthur Riley, Black Liturgies

Hearing God's voice is an act of faith, regardless of what anyone tells you. No experience of God will ever take you out of the realm of faith, no matter how dramatic it may be. On our best days, our minds are processing a multitude of voices, and our hearts are a deep ocean of past experiences, present concerns, and future hopes and fears. Our body holds every day of our lives within its cells, and our base personalities are searching for control in their unique way. It's a wonder we are able to live our lives at all, let alone communicate with the divine. Yet somewhere in the midst of it all, there is faith. I wish this pilgrimage into communion with God was cut and dry, clean and simple, concrete and definable, but it's not. There isn't anything simple about it. For some, it's terrifying to believe that God would actually speak to them. For others, they could use a little more fear and trembling every now and then to mix in with their over-confidence. There is no way to walk this out perfectly. There's no way to find absolute assurance, and there's no one in the world who has this nailed down. There are no experts when it comes to hearing God's voice. Don't let anyone tell you otherwise. If someone claims to hear God with infallibility, then I would quickly walk the other direction. A little doubt is not only normal, but it is necessary.

Throughout history, countless spiritual giants have encountered serious battles with doubt and uncertainty: St. Augustine, John of the Cross, Teresa of Avila, Meister Eckhart, John the Baptist, Thomas, Peter, and numerous others all experienced periods of serious questioning and wavering. Doubt is a powerful driving force that often propels us *toward* God and not away from Him. In contrast to oversimplified exhortations to "just believe" that seem to give birth to presumption, doubt compels us to journey beyond the realm of familiar paradigms. In this way, doubt can rescue us from the trappings of an insincere and shallow faith. A significant step into deeper spiritual waters happens when we see doubt as a gift to be celebrated and cherished.

We exist in Him, through Him, and for Him. Our hearts were created to relate to Him, express ourselves in His presence, and then expect to experience His expression in return. This is home for our soul. Somewhere in our DNA, we know our true calling is to walk in the Garden with God. Therefore, you would think that the most natural thing in the world would be for us to hear Him.

If we take the origins of humanity seriously, then it would not be a stretch to say that it's more normal to abide in Him than to go to the grocery store. We were designed, crafted, and molded for union with God. Yet we live within the tension of the *now* and the *not yet*. We dwell in the space between the resurrection and the return. We will, then, experience this wondrous relationship with God as a kaleidoscope of faith, doubt, fear, and courage. It is important that we discuss how to navigate this tension in a healthy way, giving honor to the complexity of it all.

In a spirit of self-compassion, let's embrace the notion that doubt is an intrinsic aspect of the human experience and not a failure of which we should be ashamed. As we experience doubt, we can reframe it as an inevitable part of our spiritual journey and one that can serve us well. Doubt, when embraced in a healthy manner, can be a catalyst for cultivating authenticity, bravery, and moral strength. Rather than shying away from doubt, let's view it as a powerful invitation to foster a deeper and more nuanced faith that is rooted in humility.

"I came to realize that doubt was a companion, every bit as resilient and persistent as faith, and she wasn't going away. I realized that she had some things to teach me, and I decided that since I couldn't shut her up or drive her away, I might as well learn from her. She has turned out to be a tough but effective teacher and a difficult but faithful friend."[36]

One struggle that many people deal with is the belief that doubt is sin. I strongly disagree with this sentiment. Henry Drummond, a Scottish evangelist and writer, clarifies well the difference between doubt and unbelief. "Christ never failed to distinguish between doubt and unbelief. Doubt is 'I can't believe.' Unbelief is 'I won't believe.' Doubt is honesty. Unbelief is obstinacy. Doubt is looking for light. Unbelief is content with darkness."[37]

My husband, Craig, has often taught about the places in the Gospels we see Jesus respond to doubt. He says that Jesus either: 1). ignores it; 2). instructs and teaches into it; or 3). provides tangible proof.

1. Jesus ignores it or lets it be. We read in Matthew 28:16-17, "Now the eleven disciples went to Galilee, to the mountain to which Jesus had directed them. And when they saw him they worshiped him, but some doubted." And then He continues with what we call the Great Commission. The text doesn't reveal how Jesus responded, if He responded at all, to the doubt of some. He just carried on. And at times, we can, too. We can just carry on with our doubt in the presence of the resurrected Christ in us, trusting that He knows and that He's not flustered by it.

2. When doubting, sometimes Jesus will instruct and teach. In the gospel of Luke, chapter 24, we read about 2 disciples who are on their way to Emmaus talking with each other about all that had happened with and to Jesus. While they were talking and discussing together, Jesus drew near and went with them. But their eyes were kept from

---

36   Brian D. McLaren, *Faith After Doubt: Why Your Beliefs Stopped Working and What to Do About It* (St. Martin's Publishing Group, Kindle Edition, 2022),xiii.
37   Henry Drummond, "Dealing with Doubt," as quoted in *Workday Prayers* by Timothy Jones (Loyola Press, 2000).

recognizing Him. And He said to them, "What is this conversation that you are holding with each other as you walk?"

They proceed to tell Jesus all that had happened. They finish by saying in verse 24, "'Some of those who were with us went to the tomb, and found it just exactly as the women also had said; but Him they did not see.' And then He said to them, 'You foolish men and slow of heart to believe in all that the prophets have spoken! Was it not necessary for the Christ to suffer these things and to come into His glory?' Then beginning with Moses and with all the Prophets, He explained to them the things written about Himself in all the Scriptures" (NASB). How kind of Jesus! Yes, He calls them foolish ones, but I like to think He did that with love in His heart, a twinkle in His eye, and a grin on His face. And then He proceeded to instruct them by interpreting the Scriptures for them regarding all that they had witnessed. Amazing response to doubt from our Lord.

3. And finally, in the midst of our doubt, Jesus just might provide tangible proof. We read in John 20 the story of Thomas who said, "Unless I see in his hands the mark of the nails, and place my finger into the mark of the nails, and place my hand into his side, I will never believe." And what did Jesus do? Eight days later, He showed up, invited Thomas, who was filled with doubt, to touch His wounded hands and side. He simply says, "Do not disbelieve, but believe" (John 20:27 ESV).

Jesus shows three unique responses to our doubt: He lets it be, He teaches us, or He provides tangible proof. Never do we see Him harshly condemning the one who doubted. Usually the one who condemns us for doubting is ourselves.

The origin of the word *doubt* reveals its intrinsic duality, as it stems from the words "duo" and "double." Doubt embodies the psychological tug-of-war between belief and skepticism. The dichotomy of these opposing perspectives—one driven by faith, the other by questioning—can generate an uneasy feeling as if something is wrong, since we are prone to desire clarity and control. Yet we live in a day where too many things are prematurely clarified and therefore minimized and flattened. As we give respect to the spaces where the embrace of mystery is required, we can begin to see where there is room within the mystery of God for faith and doubt to dwell together. Hearing God's voice is certainly an area where mystery must be embraced. In fact, I've come to believe that doubt of God's voice can be the beginning of real encounter. If you believe God is speaking to you but you are unsure, or if your heart is struggling to accept that what you're hearing is His voice, I suggest you put it on the imaginary table in front of you instead of throwing the moment away. Remain aware of God's presence, focused upon Him with love. In this space, you can now talk about it, giving your heart permission to lean in rather than shutting the door and walking away. This holds the questioning within the context of love and intimate relationship, rather than allowing it to become frustrated obstinance and unbelief. Evaluating what you think He may be saying is an important aspect to this whole journey. If we just grab our first sense of hearing words from God and run with our initial assumptions, we will usually get ourselves in trouble. God is often inviting us into an ongoing conversation that is to go continually deeper and wider within our soul.

In the daunting passage of James 1:5-6, we read, "But if any of you lacks wisdom, let him ask of God, who gives to all generously and without reproach, and it will be given to him. But he must ask in faith without any doubting, for the one who doubts is like the surf of the sea, driven and tossed by the wind. For that man ought not to expect that he will receive anything from the Lord, being a double-minded man, unstable in all his ways."

The first sentence of this passage lets us know the topic at hand—specifically asking for wisdom. In the original language, *giving* is emphasized as an attribute of God. So another translation might be, "Ask of the giving God," or ask of "God the giver."[38] The doubting, then, is in reference to doubting God Himself as the giver of wisdom. It's not referring to all kinds of doubt, or doubt in all circumstances. This passage is of great value in our conversation of doubt, because it highlights our need for wisdom. It draws a very clear line that God is, and always will be, the Wisdom-Giver. So in the midst of doubting His intimate voice in our lives, we can trust that the Wisdom-Giver will indeed walk with us through our uncertainty. We need wisdom far more than we need certainty, anyway.

If this conversation was about prophesying to another person/people, or hearing God's voice on behalf of others, it would be focused on testing and weighing and the accountability of community. Our personal journey of hearing God's voice is much more intimate and, therefore, even more nuanced. Faith in this private, intimate place is more challenging for many, because we don't often have the multitude of voices bringing confirmation. We can begin to wonder if we're losing our minds or have gone off the deep end. The same testing and weighing principles are helpful here, so let's run through them briefly.[39]

If you want some helpful boundary lines in discerning God's voice, His leading, His movement or expression, you will benefit by having a few markers to measure it by. These markers are ones that have been suggested by trustworthy theologians and have been proven helpful from numerous practitioners.

The number one marker is, of course, the person of Jesus. Do

---

38   M. R. Vincent, *Word Studies in the New Testament, Volume 1* (Charles Scribner's Sons, 1887), 725.

39   If you would like a more thorough discussion on the prophetic that includes a chapter on testing and weighing, please read my book *Reframing the Prophetic*. We offer a full, indepth online course on the topic as well.

we sense the essence of Christ Jesus, His character, values, and priorities? Can we imagine the Jesus we see in the Sermon on the Mount speaking these things to us? Can we feel His DNA? Is He glorified? Is what we're hearing leading us toward Jesus or not? Can we hear, see, taste, and discern the mission and the purposes of Christ through this moment? He is the Word made flesh.

The subsequent markers are:

2. The marker of the Gospel (see 1 Corinthians 12:3). Does the essence of what I believe I'm receiving from God align with the Gospel? Does it point to the Gospel, uphold the Gospel, and stand in agreement with the whole Gospel message? Does this moment somehow "preach" the Gospel in its essence? Does it carry the Spirit, the purpose, and the heart of the Gospel?

3. The marker of love (see 1 Corinthians 13). Does this encounter carry love in its essence? Does it uphold the call and the intent of love, and does it point to the eternal love of God? Does this revelation draw attention to Love, Himself?

4. The marker of community. How would this moment of experiencing God's communication hold up within the context of community? Can it withstand the spotlight of many eyes and ears who know and love you?

It's worth saying that you will be wrong. You will, at times, be absolutely certain it was the Lord, and you will discover that it wasn't really Him. I understand that this is extra challenging for those who want assurances, but there's no avoidance of our humanity. In my younger years, I was so distraught about being wrong that I foolishly tossed out the proverbial baby with the bathwater. In my flimsy, over-simplified and over-confident response to faith, I thought that if I was wrong on one portion of it, I was wrong on it all.

I've heard many followers say similar things on the heels of mistaking another voice for God. "Well, if *that* voice wasn't God's voice then I don't know His voice at all." This is, of course, fear and insecurity speaking. At the end of the day, it's utter nonsense to presume that you had His voice completely figured out. On that presumption, you are certain to fall prey to distorted beliefs and disappointments of all kinds. Being wrong about God's voice isn't the problem in this scenario. The true mistake is the pride in the original assumption that you knew His voice well enough to never be wrong in the first place.

As we relate to God, we must relate in humility, which means being aware of our complete dependence upon Him, including our ability to hear Him, perceive Him, or discern Him. Humility demands that we remain teachable, regardless of how much we think we already know. It also sets our hearts at ease within our weaknesses and mistakes. As Andrew Murray says, "Humility is simply the disposition which prepares the soul for living on trust."[40] We really can trust Him in our misunderstandings and not be surprised by the mistakes. He knows our frailties and loves us passionately. When we think it's all up to us to figure it out, we will feel terribly insecure and fearful. But when we can trust that He is the one teaching us how to relate to Him and we are safe in His love, this humility will be freeing.

> *"Absolute, unceasing, universal humility must be the root disposition of every prayer and every approach to God as well as of every dealing with man: and that we might as well attempt to see without eyes, or live without breath, as believe or draw nigh to God or dwell in His love, without an all-pervading humility and lowliness of heart."[41]*

---

40   Andrew Murray, *Humility* (Start Publishing LLC, Kindle edition, 1895), 58.
41   Andrew Murray, *Humility* (Start Publishing LLC. Kindle Edition, 1895), 60.

Humility hosts the company of both doubt and trust. It makes room at the table for paradox, knowing we often feel many things at once. We can indeed feel nagging doubt and still choose to trust, over and over again. Trust that we do hear Him, trust that His heart is always present and engaged, and trust that He has already and permanently drawn near regardless of what turmoil is going on within. In the end, doubt becomes the invitation that can lead to our transformation if we keep our heart from bitterness and keep moving forward.

Practice

Sit quietly before God in prayer and hold the idea that you have been wrong about His voice at some point (or many points) in your life. Pay attention to how this feels. Do you sense anxiety rising in your heart? Sit with it, and interview the anxiety. What are you scared of? Listen to the response that rises up, and hold that before the Lord. Remind your soul that He is big enough to guide you, even when you miss it. This is not all on your shoulders. Remind your soul that you can trust the Lord to re-direct you, to speak to you again and again, and to guide your heart into truth.

Reflection Questions

1. What is your relationship with doubt? What do you usually do when doubt shows up? Do you avoid it, wrestle with it, or try to silence it?

2. Can you sense the difference between doubt and unbelief? How would you put this in your own words?

3. Can you recall a time when doubt actually led you to deeper clarity or insight?

4.   What would happen if you allowed yourself to sit with questions rather than rush to answers?

5.   How does doubt affect your ability to trust—yourself, others, or God?

Chapter 11
Interpreting God

Over the last few decades, I've had the opportunity to connect with and minister to diverse people groups from around the world. Each year, I've had the privilege of visiting a dozen or more countries, inviting me to engage with cultures that were previously unfamiliar. These experiences have not only marked me forever, but they have also gifted me with life-long friendships from various nations across continents. These treasured connections have continuously challenged and expanded my cultural presuppositions, to put it mildly. I've often felt as though the veil was pulled back, exposing the matrix that defined my perceived reality. Every time this happens, I find it both humbling and simultaneously exhilarating.

Culture defines how we interpret everything. And I do mean everything. How I understand each and every conversation I engage with, how I filter non-verbal communication, how I interpret actions, atmospheres, grunts, groans, and tears is molded by my culture from the moment I take my first breath. In the United States, we consider staring at someone for any length of time to be either rude or romantic behavior. But in China, this action isn't considered either. For me to go to China and accuse someone of rudeness or flirting based on my cultural filter would be unfair, to say the least. In India, when citizens bob their head side to side, they are communicating something similar to the western head nodding up and down.

In Syria, it's considered polite to say "no thank you" when your host offers to feed you. When they offer again, you may graciously decline another time. Sometimes, this will happen a third time before you may accept their offer for food. It could be that you're very hungry and you were actually invited over for dinner, but this back and forth conversation will still be expected.

When our Syrian friends first came to visit us, I was absolutely befuddled when I invited them to the dinner table and they declined. I had cooked for hours, and all the food was on the table ready to be served, yet they declined my invitation to the table. I was taken aback, to put it lightly, and had to fight off feeling a bit offended that they were rejecting my dinner. They sat there watching our family eat dinner with forlorn looks on their faces and went to bed hungry. The next day, they immediately accepted my invitation to breakfast and proceeded to explain that we were supposed to keep asking! To say that we lost each other in translation was an understatement.

Everything is interpreted. Every word another person speaks, every action, every facial expression, every hand motion, and every gasp or sigh is tossed into the air awaiting interpretation by another human.

Can you imagine how drastically this affects our understanding of God? Will I interpret His silence as rejection, or think suffering in the world is a sign of His evil character? Do I see nature as an expression of His glory or a burden for us to care for? Do I interact with nature as utilitarian objects for my consumption? Do I feel the sting of loss and interpret this pain as cruelty from God? Are goosebumps a sign of God's love for me? Is playing a pipe organ holier than bagpipes?

Our understanding of God's communication is significantly influenced by numerous factors that shape our perception and interpretation. Consider the multitude of personal filters we each possess, such as cultural background, past traumas, and unique personalities. All these factors, and many, many more, have an impact on how we process the world around us. Additionally, the conclusions we draw from the information we receive continue to evolve even after we've filtered and processed. As a result, our interpretations of divine communication are deeply complex, reflecting the intricate interplay of our experiences, beliefs, and emotional landscapes.

Every time we interact with God in any way, we are interpreting that interaction and applying some kind of meaning to it. Sometimes our interpretations and meanings may be accurate, and sometimes they may not be. This is absolutely impossible to avoid. From the moment we experience anything, our human, habitual response is to ask, "What does this mean?" When this question instantly and subconsciously appears in our soul, our brain begins to search our previous experiences to find a comparison to what this is most *like*. All we have to draw on is our own lived experience, which is obviously limited. We usually come to instant conclusions that are often flawed. The meaning we attach to things then creates the emotions we feel in response.

If my husband mentions that he wants to clean the house when he gets home from work and I apply the meaning that he's upset with me for not cleaning it already (because that may have happened quite often in my childhood), I will have the emotions that go along with that meaning and respond to him accordingly. But what if he only meant that he wanted to take care of the cleaning so that I wouldn't have to do it before he returned home? We will always apply meaning to other people's words. Sometimes we'll be accurate, and sometimes we won't. It's a common struggle within every relationship. Toss in the cross-cultural dynamic and the misunderstandings multiply by the thousands.

We can't *not* apply meaning, but we can learn to become more aware of the meaning we're applying to things. Learning to pause in between communication and applying meaning can be life changing on so many levels. Just a small pause for reflection creates room in which we can remind ourselves that our first assumptions could possibly be wrong. That recognition gives us space to ask more questions for clarity. Learning how to recognize the meaning we're applying to things and hold the meanings loosely until we have a more complete understanding is imperative for all healthy relationships. The more we can grow in self awareness for the sake of stewarding our interior landscape, the more healthy we will become as humans. When that happens, our relationships with others will become more healthy, which includes our relationship with God. When we jump to conclusions and presume that we know more than we do, we will always get ourselves in trouble.

God's interaction with His prophets often begins with God asking them a question. *He's opening a conversation.* The prophet responds, then God continues, and the back and forth discussion becomes a complex and nuanced interaction with meanings that we are still unpacking today. When God speaks, He is *always* opening a conversation. This sounds like it should be obvious, but it's not. How often do we think we've heard something from God and instead of remaining in the conversation, we jump to a million conclusions and presume we know what He's speaking and therefore doing.

Oh, what wisdom we miss when we leap to conclusions

prematurely! The invitation is always to remain in the conversation with God as curious and humble as a four year old. Four year olds don't have much presumption. They do not assume they understand things already. They have a much better grasp on what they do *not* know than most adults. Knowing what we don't know seems to be challenging for most grown ups. Maybe that's because it requires true humility and genuine, honest, self awareness. When we embrace the reality of all that we do *not* truly know, we are invited into deeper trust and childlike surrender, asking far more questions than having answers. Remaining open minded, open hearted, and full of wonder is always the invitation when God speaks.

One of the most difficult things to interpret is silence. There are many kinds of silences in human relationships. The difference between the silence of a cold shoulder and the silence of a quiet evening reading books together is tangible. The atmosphere of an angry silence is dramatically different from the silence that invades a home after the funeral is over. The peaceful silence of a mother holding a sleeping baby is miles away from the silence one might feel in solitary confinement.

In Genesis 22, we see the story of God asking Abraham to sacrifice his son, Isaac, as a burnt offering. God speaks the instructions in verse 2 of the story, but doesn't speak to him again until that last fateful moment, way down in verse 11 and 12. Most of us know the end of the story before we read the shocking words in verse 2, so it saves us from the emotion that Abraham may have experienced. It isn't pleasant to meditate on Abraham's journey up the mountain, so we usually just skip to the end and wrap a beautiful, spiritual bow on it. It's almost unbearable to ponder this father's emotional state as he set out that morning, with only this command from God echoing in his soul: "Take your son, your only son Isaac, whom you love, and go to the land of Moriah, and offer him there as a burnt offering on one of the mountains of which I shall tell you."

I bet those verses between 2 and 11 felt like an eternity. Try to imagine what was happening within Abraham's mind and emotions. Could you allow yourself to slightly connect with just a twinge of the gut wrenching agony? If it was me, I know I would be desperately asking God a million questions every step up that mountain. There would be begging, tears, and raw panic. Only to be met by silence. What was that silence like for Abraham? Was Abraham sick to his stomach as God remained quiet in the face of his pleading? Was Abraham begging God for mercy as he took his son, bound him, and laid him on the kindling only to be met with more silence? At the very last moment, Abraham finally heard the angel of the Lord say, "Do not lay your hand on the boy." Can you imagine the depth of Abraham's relief? Goodness gracious, I could sob just thinking about it.

The silence of God in between these two encounters must have been excruciating. Abraham probably interpreted this silence in a multitude of ways along the path. It's human nature. But the point of the story isn't about testing Abraham. The point of this particular story is that God is not a God who asks for child sacrifice. Other nearby cultures believed their gods demanded child sacrifice, so this command would not have been altogether surprising to Abraham, even though there would be no diminishing its devastation. This whole story is about God revealing His true character to Abraham, showing His son how different He was from the other gods. This was a critical paradigm shift that would take some time to unfold.

Wrestling with God's silence was an important part of Abraham's transformation. Learning to walk with the silence of God was part of the unfolding that was only understood in the aftermath. We will indeed walk with silence as we walk with God. What if God knew it would take an extreme measure for Abraham to wake up to the true, otherworldly love of God?

The book of Job offers us an intriguing story of a man in immense suffering. His well-intentioned friends offer him all the advice any human could possibly handle, all while God remained silent. We read chapters and chapters of these supposed friends jabbering on and on with all of their made up interpretations of God's actions, all the while God is listening in silence. Job's friends interpreted the silence of God as a sign that Job must have committed a significant sin. They offered lengthy speeches accusing him of hidden wrongdoing, essentially trying to explain God's silence as a form of punishment.

Their interpretations, however, were later revealed by God to have been incorrect. He did not take kindly to their assumptions. The next several chapters are a record of God starkly and soberingly reminding Job and his friends just how all knowing, all powerful, and wholly majestic He is. He doesn't explain why He has done what He has done, or hasn't done what He hasn't done. In fact, He doesn't defend Himself at all. But the reminder of who God is, and who Job is not, left Job with one conclusion: "I have uttered what I did not understand, things too wonderful for me, which I did not know" (Job 42:3 ESV). Then God turns to these unhelpful friends and says, "My anger burns against you and against your two friends, for you have not spoken of me what is right" (verse 7).

Throughout the whole story, we watch in wonder as this good man goes through severe loss, sickness, and devastation. We see him being crushed into dust, then dazed in grief. He was in tornadic disorientation and disillusionment while God remained silent. But Job would not walk away. He also didn't pretend as though everything was okay. He was wounded on every possible level, and all he could do was crumble under the weight of unbearable pain as he listened to his friends try to interpret God. Denial was not a luxury he allowed himself. There was no escaping the trauma that swarmed him. He was shell-shocked and confused, he was angry and wished he had never been born. He yelled at God and expressed his pain honestly, yet he would not curse God and leave.

When God finally spoke, He set Job straight by unveiling the universe piece by piece. He spent chapters and chapters revealing to Job all that he didn't know, couldn't know, and would never understand. But He still said that His servant Job did what was right. He didn't condemn him for his anger, his confusion, or his pain. It is pretty clear that confusion and lack of understanding—accompanied by the corresponding emotions—aren't a problem for God. But He didn't take kindly to the friends drawing shallow conclusions with wise-sounding and presumptuous explanations on God's behalf. In a world in which we push away confusion as quickly as possible and end up arrogantly drawing false conclusions to feel as if we are in control, this whole scenario is very convicting. The religious friends of Job presumed to know what they didn't truly know about God's motives and intentions. They interpreted God incorrectly, and He didn't like it.

I feel compassion for Job's friends, probably because I've been in their shoes and said some very similar things. Things that sounded wise to my own ears, until God called them foolish and ignorant. I have confidently interpreted God only to find out how terribly wrong I was more times than I want to admit. Just as the disciples were utterly confused when Jesus told them to "eat my flesh," we will regularly find ourselves befuddled over perceived actions or inactions of God.

Can we learn to remain in confusion, rejecting denial or oversimplified shallow explanations, while still remaining in the conversation? What does it require of us to experience God's silence without offense rising in our hearts? Can we refuse to walk away when others claim

God has abandoned us? Can we hear something downright terrifying from the lips of Jesus but trust Him anyway?

This is not simple faith. This is gut wrenching, nail biting, heart sinking determination to trust when nothing makes sense. This is the courageous willingness to sit in confusion while refusing to pretend that you know what you don't know. This is the utter rejection of the arrogance of presumption, assumption, and over confidence. This is the stuff that destroys reputations, because it causes us to remain silent when everyone wants us to have something profound to say. It's also the logic-defying passion to know Him more than to understand Him. It's a rejection of the kind of wisdom that gets us on stages and in Christian spotlights, grabbing hold of a much deeper wisdom that finds peace laying at His feet, all the while being clothed with a million doubts and unanswerable questions. Yes, there's nothing simple about it.

We can't give up trying to interpret God.[42] It's the essence of all communication, and communication is the core construct of all relationships. But we can learn to hold our interpretations loosely, humbly, and in context of the universe, remembering all that we don't know and couldn't possibly understand. As we yearn to hear His voice, may we see the difference between seeking knowledge from God, grasping for understanding, and simply seeking to know Him. May we find the courage to remain in the conversation, even when our hearts are lost in translation.

---

42   Along these same lines is the practice of dream interpretation. *God Dreams* by Tania Harris is one of the first books I have found that tackles the issue of dream interpretation in a very balanced, theological, and honest way.

Practice

Sit quietly and take some deep breaths, centering yourself in God's presence. Pray through this Rainer Maria Rilke poem slowly three times. After the first reading, pause and sit in silence, allowing the words to rest in your heart. Pray this through a second time, paying close attention to what stands out to you. Sit with that specific word or phrase and reflect more deeply about what it means to you in this moment. Pray it through a third time allowing the words to go even deeper.

I believe in all that has never yet been spoken.
I want to free what waits within me
so that what no one has dared to wish for
 may for once spring clear
without my contriving.
If this is arrogant, God, forgive me,
but this is what I need to say.
May what I do flow from me like a river,
no forcing and no holding back,
the way it is with children.
Then in these swelling and ebbing currents,
these deepening tides moving out, returning,
I will sing you as no one ever has,
 streaming through widening channels
into the open sea.[43]

---

43   Rainer Maria Rilke, *Rilke's Book of Hours: Love Poems to God* (Berkley Publishing Group, 1996), 46.

Reflection Questions

1. What does it look like for you to stay in the conversation when you're confused or disoriented?

2. Can you name what silence might be creating in you rather than what that silence is withholding?

3. What does faithfulness look like when God's presence isn't obvious or affirming?

4. Are you willing to embrace mystery without letting it drive you into despair or cynicism?

5. Can you pinpoint what you may be able to describe as "an extreme measure" God enacted in order to wake you up to His love?

Chapter 12

Incarnation

The Apostle Paul, known also as Saul of Tarsus, was much more than a devout Jewish lad. Both historians and theologians suggest he was raised in a highly religious household where his parents faithfully adhered to ancestral Jewish traditions. It is likely that young Saul was seen as a scriptural prodigy. Every indication from what we know about him implies he was a remarkably talented child. He had a fluent understanding of biblical Hebrew. He conversed in Middle Eastern Aramaic and was proficient in both the spoken and written forms of Greek, demonstrating a remarkable aptitude for quick learning. His knowledge of the Bible seemed effortless and embodied by all accounts. He was brilliant.

For Saul, the Bible wasn't merely a collection of passages of wisdom and instructions; it was the story of his people. It was a tale that echoed through his faith and his life, shaping his every movement, every word, and his reason for living. As a child, his reading and entertainment would have been the stories of Moses and Elijah. He would have soaked himself in the tales of God parting the Red Sea or Elijah challenging the prophets of Baal, relishing in the story of God sending fire down from heaven. He would have repeatedly heard about that terrifying moment God appeared on the mountain top in thunder and lightning. He didn't need a superhero to capture his imagination of righteous victory. He had the stories of Ezekiel and Isaiah encountering God on His throne.

Saul was not just waiting for the fulfillment of the promised Messiah—he was actively and passionately doing everything in his power to keep his religion pure until the Messiah came. He worked tirelessly to guard the faith and to cut down all branches that would hinder or defile the traditions of his ancestors.

Saul worshiped the Almighty, Majestic One. He worshiped and served the God of Isaiah 6. In this intense description of the throne room, Isaiah saw the seraphim flying around with their six wings, two of which had to cover their eyes from the holiness that was before them. These seraphim were compelled to continually cry out, "Holy Holy Holy is the LORD of hosts" (verse 3) causing the building to shake at the voice of the Almighty. This encounter left Isaiah in utter shambles, believing he was about to die from the weight of what he was seeing. He understandably screamed, "I am ruined! I am unclean! I am unworthy to have seen the King of Kings!"

This is the God that Saul knew. He had quite possibly laid in bed at night imagining what it would have been like to have been in the room when Solomon's temple was finally finished and the people were officially dedicating the temple as the house of God. As the story goes, the Israelites had all the sacrifices done to perfection, the priests were dressed in their holy garments, and every single Israelite was standing at attention, not knowing what was about to happen. Then God came down in power and quite literally moved into His new house. All the people of Israel saw the fire come down and the glory of the Lord remain in the temple. Thousands and thousands of Israelis put their faces in the dirt, barely able to comprehend what they were witnessing (see 2 Chronicles 7). Ohhh, the glory of that temple! This is the place where heaven and earth met! This building was the only physical location the holiness of God dwelt amongst man, and therefore, was the most sacred place on earth. The temple was the center point of Israel's entire way of life.

Yes, Paul loved the fear of the Lord. He was intimately acquainted with the knee-knocking tremble, and it was exhilarating. He had given his whole life to protect the faith of his people, the traditions of his ancestors, and the way of the children of God. He was not going to let anyone threaten the truth.

Then on that fateful Damascus road, he bumped right into the Voice. As a light like he had never seen before shone all around him and knocked him to the ground, he asked the question, "Who are You, Lord?" It seemed as if he was afraid of the answer. *Could this be the One whose name I cannot speak out loud? Could this possibly be the glory of the One Isaiah spoke of? Yes, yes it must be. This is Him, this is Yahweh. I may perish this very moment.*

Then came the Voice.

"I am Jesus whom you are persecuting" (Acts 9:5 ESV).

Saul's brain must've exploded into a million pieces. He knew it was Yahweh, he knew this was the Holy One of Israel. He was already trembling, afraid, and undone. The revelation of the same glory that filled Solomon's temple on the inauguration day, the Holy One of Israel who encountered Elijah and Moses on the mountain tops, the

One who parted the Red Sea, the One the Seraphim declared "Holy, holy holy"... *this* God became *human*? How could this be? Humans are dirty, defiled, and unworthy. This man, Jesus, claimed to be the temple of God. It was the most blasphemous thing he had ever heard. But now, here in this apocalyptic moment, he finds out it's all true.

Philippians 2 says that God the Son never stopped being fully God. He appropriated human flesh to Himself while His majesty remained undiminished. In a shocking turn of events, the holiness of God clothed Himself with muddied humanity. Embodied holiness, purity, and love took on embodied fear, guilt, and shame. This union, as described by Edward Irving, is the "most violent of all contradictions."[44]

In this extraordinary convergence, the holiness of God takes our fallen nature upon Himself, and the war begins. As Jesus became human, a confrontation arose between perfection and brokenness, between God and human nature, between love and fear, humility and pride, holiness and impurity. Something would have to give. The outcome would either witness majesty defiled by sin or the birth of a new humanity.

The cross and resurrection of Christ brought redemption, but that was the crescendo, the final blow. The reconciliation really began the moment Mary became pregnant. Just as Jesus did not become leprous when He touched the leper, He would not become contaminated by humanity. His glory would transform us, minute by minute, breath by breath, every moment He lived on this earth. He entered into our wounded human existence, and while wearing our humanity, He steadfastly refused to be what we had become. Inside of our skin, carrying our *essence*, He beat His way forward, blow by blow. He entered into fallen human existence and refused to be "fallen" in it. Through 33

---

44   Edward Irving described the incarnation as "the most violent of all contradictions" in a sermon delivered on July 10, 1827 to a society focused on distributing Gospel tracts.

years of blood, sweat, and tears, through crucifixion and in the power of the Holy Spirit, He carved out the path of redemption. That is the atoning work of Jesus Christ! The Word made flesh.

He lived in perfect oneness with the Father *as a human*, carrying Mary's DNA in His bones, breaking every barrier, tearing down every wall, conquering every shadow. He opened the way for us to live in oneness with our Creator while wearing our skin. The incarnation was the starting point of the full redemption of our identity as humans. It's the most scandalous transformation of all; holiness incarnating the broken, and transforming us into His image.

It's the beginning of humanity being clothed with the Creator Himself. Human history has never been the same! Light will forever shine out of the darkness.

Jesus *is* the Word of God. He is where heaven and earth have collided, and then colluded. His existence will forever speak the loudest word. As we seek to commune with God, to listen for God in all the ways He speaks, we must first and always be listening to the life and existence of Christ. The incarnation of Christ turns the whole world into a burning bush. Everything within me and everything around me can point to this Word if I have eyes to see and ears to hear.

In 1 Corinthians 6:12-20, Paul is teaching the Church about sexual immorality. In an attempt to explain why the objectification of physical intimacy is unfathomable, He compares it with the spiritual union we have in Christ. "Do you not know that your bodies are parts of Christ?" You can almost hear His exasperation! Then He goes on to say, "But the one who joins himself to the Lord is one spirit with Him." This could be literally translated as "one breath," meaning that we are breathing *with* God, in union with Him. This is every day—the gift of our existence and the reason for our being.

Our daily invitation is to continually wake up to the reality of our constant interconnectedness with God in Christ. Orienting our hearts around this scandalous truth changes our approach to hearing His voice entirely.

We are already one with Him. We exist in Him, through Him, and for Him. We live, move, and have our being within the Word made flesh. If we never hear another word from God, it would be enough.

"We might liken the depths of the human to the sponge in the ocean. The sponge looks without and sees ocean; it looks within and sees ocean. The sponge is immersed in what at the same time flows through it. The sponge would not be a sponge were this not the case. Some call this differentiating union: the more we realize we are one with God the more we become ourselves, just as we are, just as we were created to be. The Creator is outpouring love, the creation, the love outpoured."[45]

When we drill deeper into the desire to hear His voice, we discover that this thirst is for something much more profound than a transactional discussion. Every cell in our body longs for the complete fulfillment of our eternal union with God in Christ. We live in the in between, out the back door of the resurrection and the front doorstep of completeness. In this in between, our souls can and do awaken to the truth of oneness—but remaining awake to this mystery isn't easy. Our minds get distracted and our hearts wander. It's the human condition. This longing is a gift that is present within us as a reminder of our oneness with God. It's there to tap us on the shoulder again and again as an invitation beckoning us to turn our faces back to what matters most.

---

45   Martin Laird, *Into the Silent Land* (Oxford University Press, 2006).

"The desire for God is written in the human heart, because man is created by God and for God; and God never ceases to draw [humans] to himself. Only in God will he find the truth and happiness he never stops searching for: The dignity of man rests above all on the fact that he is called to communion with God. This invitation to converse with God is addressed to man as soon as he comes into being. For if man exists it is because God has created him through love, and through love continues to hold him in existence. He cannot live fully according to truth unless he freely acknowledges that love and entrusts himself to his creator."[46]

When the incarnation is the root system for our orientation of relationship with God, we find ourselves dwelling within the substance of His voice rather than searching to hear something. This is where communion with God becomes the essence of communication with God. In Jesus, divinity is forever connected with the intimate experience of being human. In Jesus, heaven itself infiltrated earth, forever lifting the veil—if we have eyes to see.

He is our God. We are His children. He is speaking. He is waiting to teach us to recognize Him. He is Spirit. He speaks in a spiritual language. And His Holy Spirit is present as our counselor and teacher. He will teach you about the anointing you have within you. Just let Him. Turn your face toward Him and LET the Holy Spirit work. That is your part. Simply believe, and let Him do His work. He WILL lead you in the journey to know His voice. He just wants you to purposely take the journey and stay on the journey. This journey will lead you to every other place you need to go. It is here that relationship with the

46   Gaudium et Spes quoted in Joshua Elzner, *Responding to the Thirst of God: 40 Days to the Heart of Love* (Independent, 2022), 7.

resurrected Christ is forged. It is here, on this journey to know His voice, that friendship with God is experienced, that Christian maturity is experienced, that the written Word of God is understood, and being led by the Spirit becomes reality. Just stay on the journey. Turn your face toward Jesus. And let the Holy Spirit do His job. He is really good at what He does.

"All of life, I truly believe,
is reunion.
Reunion with creation.
Reunion with self.
Reunion with others.
Reunion with Creator.
A coming together after being apart."[47]

---

47   Craig Westhoff

Practice

Sit quietly, breathe deeply, and center your soul. Take some time to contemplate your union with God. He is *already* with you. He is *already* near you. He is *already* present. He is *already* communicating. After a few minutes, repeat this phrase: "This moment, I choose to feel and experience my connection with God."

Reflection Questions

1. How does the with-ness and the nearness of God affect your perception of listening for Him?

2. How does the humanity of Jesus affect the way you listen for His voice?

3. What if hearing God's voice isn't a matter of striving, but of remembering? What would you want to remember today to help your experience of oneness with God?

4. If Christ's incarnation brought the beginning of new humanity, what does it mean for you to be part of that new humanity now?

Praise
for
Reframing the Prophetic

Christine is a voice I trust. This book gives fresh vision, lived wisdom and deep scriptural guidance in the one gift that fused with Love could strengthen every believer to live lives of passionate beauty. What's on offer is a way to open the eyes of our heart - the only kind of seeing that really matters eternally. I'm so grateful.

—Danielle Strickland, justice advocate, founder, Boundless Communications, Inc., author of The Other Side of Hope, The Ultimate Exodus, and Better Together

There is a great need within the charismatic church for a more mature approach to the use of spiritual gifts, especially prophecy. In this book, Christine Westhoff addresses this need, offering a wise, mature, biblically grounded guide to the practice of prophecy in various contexts. I recommend this book for those wanting to grow in prophecy themselves and those who wish to pastor this gift more effectively.

—Dr. Lucy Peppiatt,
principal, WTC Theology, UK,
author of The Imago Dei: Humanity Made in the Image of God,
Rediscovering Scripture's Vision for Women,
Unveiling Paul's Women, and Women and Worship at Corinth

Christine Westhoff is a challenging and important prophetic voice in the Church. One that keeps aligning the people of God towards Jesus. One that has stayed normal. One that has become a trusted friend. I have profited from and I strongly recommend her teaching.

—Dr. Maximilian Oettingen, director,
Loretto Community Catholic Church,
German speaking world

This is a beautifully written and comprehensive overview of the subject itself, alongside practical teaching for anyone seeking to grow in the prophetic girt personally … and the healthy interface between prophetic ministry and the local church"

—Pete Greig
Founder, 24-7 Prayer International,
Senior Pastor Emmaus Rd, England